QUESTIONS . . . . hat questions are privi . . . . rules be suspended? Who has the floor? When should a vote be held? Who can change the topic? How is chaos prevented?

ANSWER . . . If you are planning or presiding over a meeting, *The New Robert's Rules of Order* is your answer. It establishes a master organizational plan, while providing a clear explanation of parliamentary procedure—enabling you to arrange and chair a meeting with knowledge, confidence, and control.

Whether you are conferring with 5 co-workers about the day's activities, gathered with 50 associates for a seminar, or attending a sales conference with 500 people, *The New Robert's Rules of Order* should be no more than an arm's length away.

MARY A. DE VRIES has arranged and conducted hundreds of meetings of all sizes, participating in all aspects of meeting activity from budgeting to registration. She is the editor of ten books of conference proceedings and has written dozens of other works, including three Signet Reference titles: *The Practical Writer's Guide*, *The Complete Office Handbook*, and *The New American Handbook of Letter Writing*.

THE
NEW
ROBERT'S
RULES OF
ORDER

Mary A. De Vries

A SIGNET BOOK

NEW AMERICAN LIBRARY

A DIVISION OF PENGUIN BOOKS USA INC.

Copyright © 1989 by Mary A. De Vries

SIGNET, SIGNET CLASSIC, MENTOR, ONYX, PLUME, MERIDIAN
and NAL BOOKS are published by New American Library, a division of
Penguin Books USA Inc., 1633 Broadway, New York, New York 10019

First Printing, January, 1990

1 2 3 4 5 6 7 8 9

PRINTED IN THE UNITED STATES OF AMERICA

Contents

[v]

MEETING CONDUCT:
THE NEW ROBERT'S RULES OF ORDER

PART II. ORGANIZATION AND CONDUCT OF BUSINESS

PART III. MISCELLANEOUS

Preface

If you've ever attended a meeting, let alone conducted one, you know that a lot of work goes into the premeeting arrangements and that a lot of skill goes into the actual conduct of a meeting. People who have no idea what they're doing usually manage to turn a good idea or an orderly group into a chaotic spectacle. This book is for anyone who wants to avoid that embarrassment, as well as all of those who want to handle their responsibilities in meeting organization or conduct as professionally and efficiently as possible. This book, then, is for just about everyone who attends, is an officer of, or works in schools, churches, clubs, civic organizations, political bodies, government, business and industry, and virtually any other type of organization of any size.

Although meeting conduct, especially the subject of parliamentary law, is a major concern of meeting participants, committee members, and officers, there is much more to a meeting than the activity that occurs between the opening and closing gavel. Long before the meeting is called to order, a myriad of arrangements must be made. These preliminary preparations, as well as the concluding postmeeting activities, are as crucial to the success of the meeting as the actual on-the-premises conduct of the assembled group. To remind everyone of the total picture, the first part of the book gives a capsule of key premeeting and postmeeting activities such as planning, budgeting, meeting announcements, agendas, facilities selection, speaker invitations, publicity and promotion, registration, and proceedings publication.

As the title *The New Robert's Rules of Order* indicates, however, the main focus of the book is on the conduct of meetings. The second part, in fact, is a modern version of the 1893 edition of the famous *Robert's Rules of Order*, by General H. M. Robert. Most of you will agree that after nearly a hundred years, it's time to present all of the valuable rules and procedures of this century-old text in simple, easy-to-follow, contemporary English. The fact that the 1893 edition (an update of General Robert's first 1876 edition) has survived so long attests to its value and enduring importance to readers. In fact, so many millions of readers are familiar with General Robert's original content that I've retained his exact order of topics and numbering of sections. So if you're used to remembering and referring to rules by article or section number, you need not learn any new numbers or search through a different order of topics. But those of you who found the 1893 rules hard to understand and remember will no doubt welcome the fact that this new version of the complete and official 1893 text is strictly 1989-vintage prose.

A quick-reference table of rules about motions is given at the end of the book—just before the main index—so that you can turn to it immediately, without searching. Whether you're a participant in or the chair of a meeting, you may need to check a point during the meeting. The table of rules is designed to answer up to two hundred questions in parliamentary practice.

For a detailed description of the parliamentary rules, refer to the introduction to the second part of the book—"Meeting Conduct: The New Robert's Rules of Order."

While preparing *The New Robert's Rules of Order,* I benefited extensively from the advice and parliamentary expertise of Jean McCormack, research consultant and, for this project, adviser, reviewer, and problem solver. Over a period of forty years, McCormack has arranged or conducted numerous meetings and has been active in various committees in both business and social organizations of all sizes. Most recently, she served as chapter president of a national philanthropic-educational organization. I greatly appreciated her invaluable contribution. In addition, I want to thank Richard Balkin, The Balkin Agency, and Hugh Rawson, New American Library, for their ongoing assistance.

How to Use This Work

The first part of the book—"Meeting Arrangements: Practices and Procedures"—is straightforward; to find topics you can simply look at the table of contents or check the general subject index at the end of the book. The second part—"Meeting Conduct: The New Robert's Rules of Order"—is much more complex. If you follow these steps, however, you should soon become an expert in using the rules of order in actual meetings:

- Review the table of contents for Parts I, II, and III (based on the 1893 edition) carefully and try to fix in your mind the articles in each part. In Part I, for instance, Article I is "Introduction to Business"; Article II is "General Classification of Motions"; and so forth.

- After studying the article titles in the table of contents, reread them once more and glance below each one at the related sections to gain a general impression of the type of material in that portion of the text (but don't try to memorize the section titles). For example, under Article XII, "Motions," you'll see that there are eight sections (nos. 55–63). According to the titles, the text of these sections will tell you things such as how to modify or amend a motion, how to defer action, how to suppress debate, or how to suppress a question.

- Now that you have a good idea of what the three parts contain—from reading the article and section titles—read the introduction to the part of the book devoted to the rules of order. It will give a thumbnail

definition of parliamentary law and describe the plan
of the work (as shown in the table of contents).

• Next, turn to the end of the book, to the "Quick-
Reference Guide to Motions," where you'll find all
of the motions summarized in a table of rules, along
with a list of the precedence of motions and the
forms (the wording) of putting certain questions to a
vote. This quick-reference material is what you'll use
when you're in the midst of a meeting and don't have
time to search the main text for answers. But don't
try to memorize the table and lists just yet; simply
look at them so that you'll know generally what is there.

• Now go back to the beginning of the text ("Part I.
Rules of Order") and page through the entire text of
the rules, glancing at each page only long enough to
learn how much discussion is available for each topic.
Then as soon as you have time, read the entire text
slowly and carefully. Read the quick-reference section at the end of the book, which should be much
easier to use ar 1 understand after having read the
preceding text discussions.

Assuming you have followed the above steps and are at
least more familiar now with parliamentary practice than
you were before, you are ready to test your knowledge in
an actual meeting as either an attendee, an officer, or the
chair of the group. Either way, keep the book at your
side and follow these steps when a question arises:

• Check the table at the end of the book—just before
the general index—to see which rules apply to which
motions.

• Check the precedence-of-motions list in the quick-
reference section when you need to determine the
rank (higher or lower) of motions (that is, which
motion comes first).

• Check the quick-reference section examples of forms
of putting certain questions to a vote when you want
to know the proper wording of a particular question.

- If the quick-reference material doesn't solve your problem, look up the subject in the general index at the end of the book or look in the table of contents and then turn to the applicable article or section in the text in which more details are given.

If after doing all of the above you still feel overwhelmed by the details of parliamentary practice, take heart: The more you use the book—and the various indexes and quick-reference tools built into it—the easier it will become and the more you'll appreciate the fact that the rules of order are meant to be used not only by officers of important assemblies but by everyone in any type of meeting of any size.

MEETING ARRANGEMENTS: PRACTICES AND PROCEDURES

Organization
and Planning

WOULD YOU LIKE a dollar for every meeting you've attended? A *meeting* is any act of coming together or assembly by two or more persons. It isn't even necessary for the participants to be in the same room; information can be exchanged and business can be transacted by teleconference or videoconference. When most people think of a meeting, however, they visualize people gathering together in a specific location or room, usually in a somewhat organized (even if not completely formal) manner to accomplish some objective. Two or three people might meet in someone's office to discuss activity for the day, twenty people might gather in a conference room to see an advertising presentation, thirty-five people might attend a data-processing seminar in another city, or a thousand people might travel to the annual conference of a merchandising association. The examples are endless. But it's obvious that a common way of categorizing meetings is by size, from a one-on-one office meeting to a convention with hundreds or thousands of attendees. One reason for nearly always considering size in a meeting is that it has such a great deal to do with the organizational requirements, the cost, the duration, and so on. But there are other important ways to classify meetings, such as the degree of formality, the principal type of activity involved, the frequency of meeting, or the main objective. Regardless of the intent, though, a meeting should serve a useful purpose.

Is a Meeting Necessary?

One of the most crucial considerations in holding a meeting is the objective. Why do you need a meeting? Admittedly, some people don't; one gets the impression that people often meet merely out of habit and that they have lost the ability to act alone or through less time-consuming means. Some of you may remember from your science lessons in school that certain species appear to have lost abilities or attributes they used to have: Some fish living forever in deep, dark waters have lost their need for eyes and have become sightless; some land creatures formerly with wings have stopped flying and have become earthbound. Have we lost our ability to function without a meeting? No doubt you can all document cases of unnecessary meetings. But this shouldn't cloud the fact that without person-to-person contact at work and in social settings and without organized assemblies of people who have common needs and interests, a lot of activity would grind to a halt and important needs would remain unattended.

Meeting Objectives

Many meetings (such as staff meetings, committee meetings, and board meetings) may have multiple objectives: to present or exchange information, to solve a problem, to make a decision, to plan an upcoming event, to make work assignments, to investigate some matter, and any number of other concerns—all at the same meeting. Some meetings may have only one objective, but most meetings are more complex. Yet the various objectives may not be equally important. A board of directors, for instance, might meet primarily to nominate new officers, but it would also want to take care of several other matters before adjourning.

The reasons for meeting vary with the type of business or professional activity of the participants. A parent-teacher association is involved in activities that are very different from those of a computer manufacturer's sales team. The parent-teacher association might meet to discuss student events and a changing educational curriculum in its concern with educational goals and needs, whereas the sales team would be motivated by profit goals and might meet to plot sales strategy or prepare to introduce a new product.

Not only do different organizations meet for different reasons, but each organization itself could have vastly different objectives from one meeting to another. A church body on one occasion might hold a meeting to determine whether a member who violated some rule should be expelled and on another occasion would be concerned with its annual budget. A hospital committee or board might meet on one or more occasions to plan the addition of a new wing and on another occasion would want to discuss new operating-room procedures. In all of these cases, different people would probably attend each meeting. Possibly a hospital board of directors would meet with members of a planning committee to discuss the new wing, whereas the operating-room staff might go out of town to attend a seminar with other personnel from other hospitals to learn about new operating-room procedures.

The more examples we consider, the more obvious it becomes that we are dealing with an exceptionally broad subject in this book. For that reason, the examples that are mentioned here are just that—selected examples out of the thousands of possibilities. The first part of this book, then, is really a brief overview of some of the important steps to take in arranging a meeting. Each organization and each meeting will have its own unique requirements, however, and those who are responsible for the meeting arrangements must tailor procedures to fit their particular situation. (For details on the conduct of formal assemblies under the rules of parliamentary law, see the second part of the book, "Meeting Conduct: The New Robert's Rules of Order.")

Organization and Planning

Where do you start if you want to hold a meeting? Like any other project or activity, a successful meeting requires advance planning and effective organization. If you don't know where to start, take a pencil and paper and imagine that your assignment is to make a meeting blueprint or a master plan. Furthermore, assume that this will be more than a two-person office or social meeting. Perhaps it will be a departmental meeting or a seminar or something else with at least one room full of attendees.

The first thing you should do is identify everything that will go in the master plan: a general manager and a meeting coordinator, a proposed meeting chair, committees to handle the various aspects of the meeting (finance, program, site and facilities, exhibits, audiovisual and other equipment, meals and refreshments, entertainment, registration, publicity, mailings, proceedings publication, and so forth), administrative and clerical staff to process information, guest speakers, and anything else that applies to the particular meeting you want to hold.

Your master plan needs something else: evaluation or analysis before, during, and after the meeting. For this, you'll want to identify key individuals with whom you'll brainstorm. List some of the matters you'll want to discuss:

- A statement of the need for and purpose of the meeting

- A theme or title (for a conference, for example)

- An estimate of support from interested persons

- Alternative plans if the master design needs revision later

- Strategies for collecting data, monitoring progress, and evaluating success at each stage of operations

- Procedures (how will the functions be handled?)

• Strategies to motivate people and control finances and scheduling

This part of your plan, then, concerns intangible items: the planning, control, and management behind the scenes—before, during, and after the meeting. The attendees at the meeting probably won't see any of this; they'll see a meeting room properly set up for them but won't know about the advance thought, the contacts, and the staff work that made it possible. If the attendees are served lunch at the meeting, they probably won't realize that you had to decide in advance whether or not to give them lunch, that you had to contact a food-service representative, that you had to build time for this into the schedule, that you had to select the right menu and estimate the number to be served, and that you had to coordinate all of this with the Finance Committee and other involved persons. To the attendees, all of these things that they see and receive at the meeting will not appear out of the ordinary, but you know that they didn't just happen with the snap of a finger. You also know that the meeting probably would have been a disaster if you hadn't drawn up a good master plan in advance and set up the necessary controls—with backup strategies and alternative steps to take should anything suddenly go wrong.

Your master plan should specify what type of meeting you're going to have. This may change—like everything else—once a planning committee is formed and the key individuals start brainstorming. But for now, you need to get an outline ready so that the initial meeting won't wander off in a dozen directions at once. So make an effort to describe the type of meeting you visualize—including aspects that are already decided (it *has* to be a sales meeting) and those that are open to suggestions (where you'll hold the meeting)—or list a first, second, and third choice. The easy part is identifying the kind of meeting it will be. Will it be a sales meeting? A chapter meeting of your professional association? A training workshop for your departmental staff? Something else? Will the purpose be to learn something or to exchange information? To solve some problem at work? Something else? When it comes to site and related matters, more advance thought and decision making are involved. Would you prefer to meet locally or have a two-day meeting out of town with meals, transportation, and the like provided?

Your master plan certainly will have a slot in it for the place and date and, eventually, the times set for speeches, discussion, meals, and so on. All that you can do at this point, however, is list some alternatives. If you will be meeting somewhere away from the office, you will first need to select the site and find out if reservations can be made for the dates and times you prefer. After evaluating the estimated attendance, the costs, and the convenience of various sites in terms of travel and time away from work, you may need to modify your initial thoughts. So this information on your plan will be tentative (like many of the other things). Nevertheless, you want to mention everything imaginable now—knowing that more complete facts will be plugged in later—so that you won't sit down with the Planning Committee without an idea in your head or without any sort of guide to the advance work that awaits the key initiators of the meeting.

If this were to be a small, uncomplicated meeting, however, there might be no key individuals to form a planning committee—you might be a committee of one. But in that case, you would need the plan even more. Now that you have jotted down the principal areas you need to consider *in advance*—before anyone, staff or other, goes to work on arrangements—you can add details to your basic plan. Depending on what you have in mind for a meeting, some of the things mentioned above may not apply or there may be other considerations that you will want to add to your master plan.

Also, depending on the complexity of your proposed meeting, you may or may not need scheduling, budget, and other forms. But your organization probably has standard forms that are used for meetings. It may have a company budget-authorization form that you'll have to complete. Or perhaps there's an annual meeting calendar or schedule for the company that you have to check for open slots and then record your meeting on one of the open dates that is suitable for you. If your organization holds multiple meetings each year, you may be required (or want) to schedule all of your meetings in advance for the entire year. Also, you may have access to an equipment checklist on which you can check off each chalkboard, eraser, overhead projector, microphone, and so on as you order it, as it arrives, and as it's set up in the meeting room.

If your company doesn't have such meeting forms, inquire at an office-supply store for standard forms or secure a copy of a meeting planner such as the American Management Association's *Conference and Workshop Planner's Manual* (always ask for the latest edition of any book), which has everything from a sample planning schedule, budget, equipment and supply checklist, and registration form to a speaker-appraisal form and an exhibitor contract. Your local library may have books on meetings and conferences, and most well-stocked bookstores that handle business-related subjects carry such books. For a large conference or convention, such forms and checklists are a must. Even for a small meeting, a scaled-down version of such material would be invaluable to the person who has to stay on top of numerous details and supervise the assistants handling some of the arrangements.

The main thing to remember from this brief summary is that planning must precede action. Although you may be an expert at filing your ideas in your mind, it's not a good idea to rely on your memory even with simple office meetings. To be certain that you don't forget something, it's always best to jot down ideas on paper. The larger the meeting, the more formal your records must be, but anything is better than nothing. If the term *master plan* sounds too formidable for the small meeting that you want to hold, think in terms of an outline or just a simple things-to-do checklist. You can make other lists to accompany this, such as a staff-assignment checklist: meals—Roy; room reservations—Jody; and so on. Having information available in written form will be helpful not only to you but to others in case you become ill or

have another emergency that makes it impossible for you
to continue work on the arrangements.

As soon as you have at least a skeletal plan in mind,
it's time to meet with key individuals (if any) and form
committees or, in the case of a small meeting, make task
assignments for your staff. How all of this is handled
depends on your organization. Some permanent societies
require that committee appointments and the like be
handled at an organized meeting of the society through a
vote of the members present. Or someone at such a
meeting may make a motion that the chair appoint a
conference committee. (See the discussion of committees
in "Meeting Conduct: The New Robert's Rules of Order.") In an office situation, a manager or department
head might make all such decisions. Or a board of directors might appoint a conference chair, who in turn would
appoint an executive committee or planning committee
that in turn would appoint various other committees (budget, hotel, and so on).

However your organization operates and whatever authority you have to proceed alone, one person or a
committee or various people or various committees will
have to be responsible for some or all of these functions:

- Planning
- Finance
- Program development
- Speakers
- Meeting notices and agendas
- Publicity and promotion
- Registration
- Site and facilities
- Equipment and presentation aids
- Exhibits and demonstrations
- Meals and entertainment
- Minutes and Proceedings

These items are all described in the following sections. (For details on the formation of a new organization and the first and second meetings, see "Meeting Conduct: The New Robert's Rules of Order," Section 48.)

Finance

Who's in charge of the money? If your meeting is large enough to involve expenses, someone has to be responsible for the fiscal aspect of the arrangements. Although a small meeting in your office may not involve more than a cup of coffee or a soft drink—perhaps purchased out of the office petty-cash fund—a larger meeting could involve room and equipment rental, catering-service charges, transportation costs, speaker fees, printing and promotion costs, and other expenses. When a meeting involves such things, it clearly points to the need for a budget and one or more persons in charge of financial record keeping and disbursements.

Financial control can be handled in various ways depending on the type and size of meeting, the number of expense categories involved, the prior existence of a financial officer in your organization who always handles meeting finance, and any rules or regulations in your organization that specify the required procedure. But as an example, assume that you have been appointed finance chair in a national organization that's planning to hold a three-day meeting in Cleveland. What should you do? (See also "Meeting Conduct: The New Robert's Rules of Order," Section 52.)

First, you should ask for instructions from the Planning Committee or from the specific person(s) to whom you'll be reporting (such as the meeting chair or coordinator). Be certain to find out if the meeting is expected to be a money maker or a break-even event or whether it's expected to operate at a loss to the organization (not all meetings are intended to make money; some serve an indirect purpose, such as company enhancement or nonprofit, educational needs). Next you'll want to review the bylaws or other rules and regulations of your organization to see which (if any) requirements apply to financial matters in a meeting (perhaps, for example, the secretary of the organization must always approve all expenditures and the treasurer always sign all checks). As soon as you know what you may and may not do and who does what in regard to approving final expenditures and paying the incoming bills, you're ready to go to work.

If you were instructed to form your own committee and the proposed meeting is large enough to warrant other members (in addition to your own staff assistants in your office), you would begin here. Select one to three other persons to make up your Finance Committee and, if they accept the appointments, set up a meeting with them as soon as possible. This first meeting is important since you'll establish the parameters of activity and assign duties to the other members. Explain the ground rules to the others (in regard to the do's and don'ts of your organization) and then cover several other key points in this first meeting. (You may do more or less than suggested here to the extent that your own meeting differs from this example:)

- Discuss the preliminary meeting plans and schedule—proposed meeting dates and sessions, probable number of speakers, desired number of attendees, and so on.

- Give the members a list of the other committees and names, addresses, and telephone numbers of the chairs.

- Describe the duties and procedures of finance committees for previous meetings.

- Give members a copy of a budget used for a previous, similar meeting as an example.

- List the tasks and steps concerning finance that you anticipate for the upcoming meeting.

- Assign specific tasks, with priorities, to the other committee members; for example, each person may be responsible for collecting information pertaining to certain expense items (such as hotels and meals or printing and promotion) on the budget.

• Discuss any other tasks, procedures, or pertinent matters; include on-site rules and procedures (does the organization allow or will you allow registrants to cash checks or use credit cards?) as well as premeeting committee procedures.

• Set a date for the next meeting at which time members should report their activity to date and further steps should be defined.

Committee members will no doubt have certain persons on their own office staffs to help in collecting, organizing, and recording data, although each member will be responsible for his or her own assignments, and you as the finance chair will be responsible for the work of your committee.

As soon as possible make appointments to meet individually or all together with other committee chairs to collect information and to be certain that everyone is on the same track and working in unison. Speed is generally important since committees need to know their fiscal limits in order to pursue their assigned arrangements. Estimated costs, for instance, will affect decisions about what to charge for a registration fee.

If the Planning Committee has appointed a meeting coordinator, this person will help immensely in maintaining smooth, consistent operations and contacts with other committees. But in any case, you need a budget from each committee to use in preparing your own overall budget. In other words, you don't have to go to the hotel representative yourself to find out the various estimated hotel costs for the meeting; the Facilities Committee is responsible for making such hotel contacts and collecting such data. But you must incorporate the Facilities Committee's budget into your overall meeting budget. Once you have all of the committee budgets—and have worked with the committees in ironing out any related problems—

you're ready to prepare the total meeting budget to be presented to the Planning Committee for approval.

Depending on the size of the upcoming meeting, your budget may include room rental, meals and other refreshments, gratuities, entertainment, airport transportation, equipment rental, telephone, postage, stationery, addressing and mailing, printing, photocopying, speaker fees, parking, and anything else needed before, during, and after the meeting. If you set up your expense categories with a computer, you can change your figures on a moment's notice and quickly print out a revised budget at any time.

If your organization doesn't have a standard format that you must follow for the budget, devise a suitable arrangement of data, possibly like a columnar pad. List the expenses (rooms, meals, and so on) in the left-hand column and across the page have a row of expense columns. Head the first expense column "Proposed Expenditures" and head the next few columns "Revised Expenditures"; fill in your revised figures in the blank columns each time you have to change the budget. Then head the next three to six columns "Expenditures to Date"; use these columns to record how much has been spent as of certain dates. Head the final column "Total [*or* Actual] Expenditures"; there you'll record the sum of all bills paid for each category listed in the first column (meals, equipment rental, and so on). After all figures are finally available, add each column and note the total at the bottom.

Expenses	Proposed Expend.	Rev. Expend.	Expend. to Date	Total Expend.
(1)	(1)	(1) (2) etc.	(1) (2) (3) etc.	(1)

Be prepared to make revisions. Portions of the budget may not satisfy the Planning Committee. Perhaps the proposed printing expenditure looks too high to the committee, or perhaps the meals figure looks too low; in that case, you'll have to go back to the committees in charge of printing and meals and work out revised figures. Continue with this procedure until, finally, your overall budget is approved. As soon as it is, notify the other committees concerning their own categories in the budget. (You may, however, have to submit some revised budgets as certain committees advise you from time to time that their original estimates are proving to be inaccurate. To avoid a lot of this, the Planning Committee should insist that committees secure signed contracts with prices clearly defined.)

Let the other committee chairs know how much they may spend on the spot, on their own, without authorization from the Planning Committee or your Finance Committee and which expenses must be cleared first. Establish guidelines for them in regard to ordering supplies (ask for a written request with related cost estimates), prepaying vendors (don't do it unless it was agreed to in a signed contract), submission of receipts to you (all receipts by other committees should promptly go to you); and so on.

Throughout the period of meeting preparation, you will need to report regularly to the Planning Committee, indicating the work status of your committee and presenting an updated statement of income (from registrations, for example) and expenses. If your organization doesn't have a standard form, follow the example of statements submitted in previous meetings of your organization. Or simply prepare a list of income received by category (registration fees, sales of publications, and so on) and then expenses by category (supplies, speaker fees, and so on), with net profit or loss to date (total income to date minus total expenses to date). If you set up the categories on a computer, you can quickly insert new figures and print out a new statement at any time. Also, establish a procedure for recording and depositing receipts and for approving bills for payment.

Your organization may require that you immediately turn over all receipts to the accounting department or to the person designated as bookkeeper or treasurer. But you still need to keep your own records of registrations paid and to be billed as well as a current list of bills paid and due (use a computer to minimize tedious hand work and to enable you to see instant updates). The exact procedure used should be established in conjunction with the accounting department's requirements and your own need for fiscal monitoring and control. But no matter who actually does the bookkeeping, income and expenses must be recorded in the books of account according to the method required in your organization.

Be certain that everyone (on your committee and on other committees) closely reads what outside contracts require in regard to when payment is due. In other words, when does a deposit or a final check have to be drawn, and is the contract consistent with your organization's own rules and procedures? If the committees don't take care in contracting, bills may be due and payable before enough receipts have come in to cover them. Or you may have the reverse problem: it takes so long for bills to come in or for committees to submit them to you that you can't properly monitor and control the handling and reporting of income and expenses. You may even have to ask for bills in order to prepare required financial reports on schedule.

After the meeting, you will need to take care of the final unpaid bills, see that on-site or late registration fees and other receipts are deposited, and—finally—close the books for this meeting. (Again, coordinate this aspect closely with your accounting department or with the designated bookkeeper or treasurer.) After you've taken care of the last details, submit a final income and expense report to the Planning Committee.

Program Development

All kinds of organizations plan programs to present to members and invited guests as well as to the general public. Your local garden club may hold a flower show with competitive entries, judges, noncompetitive displays, guest speakers, and other features. A school may prepare a recital for parents, teachers, and the community at large. A company may provide an orientation program for new employees or a product demonstration for customers and prospects. A technical society may hold an annual conference with numerous speakers and sessions. For each of these events, some person or committee has to develop the program, and the more complex the meeting, the more that the person or committee will have to do. (See also "Meeting Notices and Agendas" in the next chapter.)

Consider again the example of a national organization holding a three-day meeting in Cleveland. This time you're in charge of program development. For a meeting of this complexity, a committee will likely be needed—it's more than one person can handle alone, at least if that person also has a full-time job elsewhere. What do you do first? Follow the example of the Finance Committee described in the previous section: review any instructions you receive from the Planning Committee, study the bylaws and any other rules and regulations of your organization, and examine the correspondence and reports of previous program committees and the printed programs they developed. Now you're ready to set up a committee. You probably will want one to three people to work with you, in addition to members of your staff at the office. As soon as your choices to serve on the committee accept their appointments, make arrangements for a first meeting.

Also follow the example of the Finance Committee's first meeting in regard to the agenda for the first program meeting: discuss preliminary plans and scheduling, give your committee members an address list of the other committees, tell them about the duties and procedures of previous program committees, show them copies of previous programs, list the tasks you anticipate for your committee, make committee task assignments (perhaps each person will be working on a certain portion of the program), and set a date for the next committee meeting. If the proposed three-day meeting in Cleveland has a coordinator (it probably does), meet with that person to establish working procedures and then meet regularly thereafter. If there's no coordinator, take the initiative yourself and open the channels to the various committees (site and facilities, meals, equipment, registration, and so on)—you'll be developing a program consistent with their activities.

Although a lot of meetings are different and have different needs and hence different planning procedures, you'll no doubt be aiming toward the preparation of an organized plan of events and all related aspects, from registration details to hotel accommodations. This plan presumably will be printed and mailed to interested persons who might attend the meeting in Cleveland. There may be another person or committee in charge of printing and mailing or each committee may handle its own printing and mailing requirements. Regardless of the practice in your organization, your task is, first, to develop a three-day program to be presented in as-yet-undetermined facilities in Cleveland.

The Planning Committee has probably suggested a theme and stated its objectives. The Finance Committee either has or will request a proposed Program Committee budget from you and, when the overall meeting budget is approved by the Planning Committee, will let you know exactly what expenses you may incur (speakers' fees, telephone and postage costs, and so on), which ones require authorization, and how to handle ongoing budget revisions. In the meantime, you can be clarifying certain program details within your own committee: If you haven't been given a specific title for the conference, what titles can your committee suggest to the Planning Committee? (The Publicity and Promotion Committee will be interested in such details also.) How would you characterize the expected audience and how will you reach it? (This may be the responsibility of the Publicity and Promotion Committee, but nevertheless you'll need to work closely with anyone who has to get the news of your program out to the selected audience.)

What is the objective of the meeting: to provide an educational program for your organization's membership and other interested parties? To provide a forum for interested persons to exchange new developments and techniques in your field or to solve problems that affect everyone in the industry or profession? Most meetings have more than one objective; in any case, the purpose for the meeting is your guide to the program—the topics for discussion that you'll set up, the speakers you'll need, and so on. It also is a key to the audience you'll contact to solicit attendance.

Time and date are two things of major importance to the Program Committee. You need to deal in specifics, not generalities. Precisely when does on-site registration begin and end? There will be chaos if your schedule isn't stated accurately. Precisely when does this or that session start and end in this or that specific room and on which day? Precisely when is there a refreshment break? Precisely when is the Tuesday luncheon speaker to be introduced and brought to the podium? Your program for each day should begin with breakfast or the first scheduled event or action; include the exact time that certain doors will open or when an information, publications sales, or registration booth will open for business. Entertainment or special events for spouses and attendees should also be included (events such as tours and dinnerdances should appeal to both men and women), as well as day-care arrangements.

Some program chairs use a ruled sheet or a columnar pad with times in ten- or fifteen-minute increments in the left-hand column (your organization, however, may have standard forms that you should use). Across the top of the page would be five columns—three for the three days of the proposed meeting and first and last columns for the day before the meeting begins and the day after the meeting has ended (some things such as transportation to and from the airport would be penciled in on those days).

Activity Schedule

Time	March 5	[March 6	March 7	March 8]	March 9

Another simple program-planning tool is a box of three-by-five-inch index cards. You can write each session (speech, workshop, and so on) on a separate card and move the cards around in different order until you're satisfied with the order of topics on each day. If you're using a computer, you can easily revise the titles of topics and their order and print out an updated schedule at a moment's notice.

You'll need a lot of brainstorming sessions with your own committee—and others—to select the best mix of topics for the workshops and other sessions, including prospective speakers. The Planning Committee may give you only a general theme and sample topics or certain essential topics that it definitely wants you to include. It will then be up to you and your committee to spell out a well-rounded mix and arrange the topics over the three days to give people clear and convenient choices for the sessions they want to attend. Some sessions may be parallel—two or more running at the same time in different rooms. This type of meeting presents a problem. Although traffic control may not be specifically your responsibility, you need to consider it in scheduling sessions to avoid bottlenecks and confusion.

It will be a miracle if you can finalize every topic and have speakers committed to handle all topics by the time you need to print and mail an advance program and registration packet. Although all program committees dislike having to state "To Be Announced" in a topic or speaker slot on a program, it may be unavoidable in some cases. If your audience is widely scattered geographically and you're mailing at the less-expensive but slower bulk-third-class rate, the program mailing may be scheduled two to three months before the meeting to reach people early enough for them to be able to register and make other arrangements to attend. Speakers may not be immediately available to give you an answer, and if they're outstanding persons, you may elect to wait for their replies rather than select someone of lesser stature who might be able to give you a fast yes or no. (For details about arrangements for speakers and for the printing and mailing of program packages, see "Speakers" in this chapter and "Publicity and Promotion" in the second chapter.)

Throughout your work in developing a program, you should report your progress regularly to the Planning Committee and work closely with the meeting coordinator (if any) or the chairs of the various committees (facilities, meals, and so on) who will be providing details to you to go in the program. The Planning Committee will probably expect you to submit a list of proposed topics and events and a tentative time-date schedule as well as a proposed list of speakers and assigned topics. The topic list must be approved before you have a program printed, and the speaker list also should be approved before you issue invitations to speakers (but follow the procedure in your organization for all of these things).

Speakers

Meeting arrangers rely on guest speakers for many types of meeting programs. A local chamber of commerce may want someone to speak about community development at a luncheon meeting. An investment firm may want several in-house employees or outside speakers to address the registrants at a seminar for investors. A national trade association may hold a major conference or convention that has numerous sessions with guest speakers. As usual, the larger and more complex the meeting, the more that you have to do to make speaker arrangements.

The person in charge of program development or the Program Committee for an upcoming meeting usually handles speaker arrangements. The Planning Committee may or may not give you instructions for this; in any case, look at the roster for previous meetings and find out whether your organization has any in-house forms you might use or adapt to your needs (forms for biographical data on speakers, their supplies and equipment needs, their travel or airport-transportation requirements, and so on). If you can't find any forms, develop something that speakers can fill out; don't rely on them to tell you everything they need. Also, if everyone fills out the same form, you'll receive more consistent information.

If necessary, develop forms for your own use. For each

topic on your program, for example, you'll want to know what special requirements are involved. What background or education must a speaker have for the particular topic? What enhancements does the topic require (filmstrips, chalkboards, audience participation, and so on)? Who are some likely candidates for speaking on a particular topic in terms of experience and education? Speaking ability?

A columnar-pad type of format will serve most purposes. In the left-hand column list each topic (with date and times). Across the top, head the various columns with the pertinent items, such as supplies needed (for speakers or for audiences), equipment needed (such as audiovisual aids), special speaker requirements (education, job experience, and so on), prospective candidates, sources of candidates (direct company contacts, speaker bureaus, directories, and so forth), and any other data you'll need to know. This type of self-designed format can be used on a computer as well. The important thing is to have some type of speaker-selection chart in front of you—something you can scan and from which you can gain a total picture of needs without fear of overlooking something.

		Requirements			Speakers	
Topic	Date-Time	Supplies	Equipment	[Etc.]	Prospects	Sources

Have each of your committee members fill in a form; you can then combine all of their suggested equipment needs, speaker-candidate suggestions, and other requirements on one master chart. Don't hesitate to ask others working on the meeting arrangements for suggestions or to use any other source you can think of to ask for speaker recommendations. Most meeting planners prefer to have personal recommendations, but if none is forthcoming, you may want to peruse the trade press for names or consult appropriate directories such as those of the National Speakers' Association or Meeting Planners International. Check your yellow pages for nearby speakers' bureaus.

If your meeting is large and complex, you may want to use more forms, such as a speaker-evaluation form. For each suggested candidate you would answer questions (if known) about the speaker's suitability for your program:

- What qualifications or credentials does the person have to speak on the proposed topic?
- Was the individual recommended by someone?
- Is the person an effective speaker?
- What speaking fee will the person expect?
- Is the person likely to be available?
- Will the person, by reputation, enhance the program?

As you study the evaluation forms, consider whether the complete roster of speakers provides the mix you want in terms of gender, age, experience, religion, race, education, and geographic representation. Not many organizations today would want to hold a meeting at which all of the speakers are white Protestant males from New York City, over age sixty, who went to the same university and who presently hold the same type of executive position. Strive for a variety that will reflect the composition of your audience.

When you have matched one or more names of prospective candidates to the topics on your selection chart, rank them in order of preference (put a *1* by your first choice, a *2* by your second choice, and so on). Then submit your list to the Planning Committee for approval. Once you have authorization to proceed, begin preparing your speaker invitations. If your organization has on file copies of previous correspondence with speakers, you can use them as a guide. Otherwise, first prepare a basic letter of invitation that will be suitable for most of your initial speaker contacts.

You might also want to prepare a speaker-information sheet. This would be a photocopied or printed information sheet—accompanied by a brochure describing your organization—telling speakers:

- The theme and title of the meeting

- The meeting dates

- The meeting location

- A capsule of the expected audience and number attending

- Your organization's policy concerning fees or honorariums

- The policy concerning expense reimbursement and transportation fees for speakers

- Other general information a speaker should know

Close with the name, address, and telephone number of someone the speaker may contact for further details. If you put all of this routine information on an enclosed summary sheet, you can confine your letters to the speakers to details pertinent to each speaker: the person's topic and any desired slant or emphasis, the date and exact time of the presentation, and so on. If you don't have a data sheet to enclose, your letter will have to be much longer and more detailed.

The correspondence from an organization to a speaker will be signed by either the Program Committee chair or the conference chair (except that a contract is usually signed by the conference chair). How many letters you write to each speaker depends on the type of meeting. The following letters are common:

- A letter inviting the person to present an address at the organization's upcoming meeting (enclose a speaker's information sheet describing the meeting, financial arrangements, and other matters, as explained above, as well as a brochure about your organization).

- A confirmation letter acknowledging the speaker's acceptance (or refusal, if that's the case), restating the facts about the speaker's presentation (such as topic, objectives, date, and time). Enclose a contract (if any) and forms for the speaker to complete, such as a biographical summary sheet and a supplies and equipment requirement checklist (see "Equipment and Presentation Aids" in the third chapter). Have space on this form for the speaker to indicate any desired room setup (see "Site and Facilities Arrangements" in the third chapter).

• A welcome letter to serve as a cover letter with the packet of information given to speakers arriving at the meeting. This packet should include materials such as a printed program, an expense form, a name tag, a map of the meeting facilities (if available), and any other material or information a speaker will need.

• Thank-you letters after the meeting complimenting the speakers on their outstanding contributions.

If you enclose a contract with your confirmation letter, ask the speaker to return it by a certain date and to send you a photograph and biographical summary, the precise title wording of the speaker's presentation (otherwise you'll be forced to put your own version of a title on the program), a list of supplies and equipment needed, including audiovisual aids and audience supplies, and an outline of the speech. If a written copy of the speaker's paper is needed for inclusion in a published book of proceedings, state the requirements (length, photographs, style, and so on) and deadline for submission (see "Proceedings" in the fourth chapter). A form that the speaker can complete (as described earlier) will make it easier for everyone. If speakers don't have a form to complete, you can be certain that some of them will forget to tell you something, and you'll simply have to write follow-up letters or make follow-up telephone calls.

A contract should be sent to a speaker in duplicate, with one signed copy to be kept by or to be returned to the speaker. Usually, such an agreement states the meeting theme, date, and location and lists the details of the speaker's presentation—such as title, time, and date—as well as any financial, transportation, billing, and other arrangements for the speaker, with terms in event of cancellation by the speaker. It should be signed by both the meeting chair and the speaker. Many organizations holding small meetings, however, consider the routine exchange of correspondence to be a sufficient understanding of the terms of the arrangement and each party's commitment (follow the practice in your organization), but a specific contract or letter of agreement is always added insurance that there will be no misunderstanding later.

Although the above steps are all important, you may do more or less depending on your particular meeting. Regardless of how much you need to do for your organization and meeting, everyone who makes arrangements for even one speaker shares one concern—the dread that there will be a late cancellation. Things happen, though, and people sometimes must bow out of a speaking engagement. Knowing that this is always a possibility, you can save yourself and your organization a lot of grief by arranging for standby speakers.

Sometimes members of the organization prepare addresses—just in case. Or outside speakers may be selected as alternates or standbys. These persons may be prepared to speak on the scheduled topic or they may have another topic to address. Standbys should receive all of the literature that a scheduled speaker would receive, so that last-minute briefing can be minimal. Any such late program changes must be announced to the attendees as soon as possible, perhaps at a breakfast gathering. If there's an information booth or a bulletin board in the lobby, post the change immediately. Finally, report such changes to the Planning Committee and be prepared to make the necessary supplies and equipment changes or any other changes necessitated by the unexpected cancellation.

Attendee Contacts

Meeting Notices and Agendas

WHEN A MEETING is large and complex—a conference, for example, with multiple sessions and numerous guest speakers—the organizers must prepare a program (see "Program Development" in the preceding chapter) and mail it, along with registration details, in advance to prospective registrants. This advance program-registration package serves as both a notice of the upcoming meeting and the agenda for the overall conference. (See also "Publicity and Promotion" in this chapter.) During the program, however, the board of directors of the organization and various committees may hold small meetings of their own to transact pertinent business. Notices of such meetings and the associated agendas are handled apart from the general meeting announcement and program. Such meetings are common everywhere, in fact, and do not occur only during a larger program open to selected participants or the general public. Every day, in social and business settings, people meet to discuss something and transact business, whether or not another larger general program is also occurring simultaneously. (The second part of this book—"Meeting Conduct: The New Robert's Rules of Order"—describes procedures for conducting meetings under the rules of parliamentary procedure.)

Perhaps you want to meet with someone in your home or office or to hold a larger organized meeting to discuss something or transact business that requires the concurrence or vote of other members of your group. To hold a meeting, you need to announce the time and the place and prepare an agenda for the meeting. If you simply want to talk to someone in your office, the notice would likely consist of a telephone call or a brief letter or memo asking the individual if it would be convenient to meet in your office at a certain time on a certain day to discuss so and so. Your agenda for this informal meeting might consist of some personal penciled notes to help remind you of points you want to make or questions you want to ask during the meeting.

But assume that it's time to hold a meeting of the board of directors of your local business association. If the bylaws of the organization specify that the secretary is to call, or announce, such meetings, and you're the secretary, you will prepare some type of formal notice. Perhaps your organization has always sent notices in the form of business letters prepared by computer. If the meeting is larger, though, possibly including the entire membership, you will probably have announcements printed, with or without a proxy. A combination notice-proxy such as the following standard form is used in many organizations:

NOTICE

Members of the Business Association are hereby notified that the next meeting of the Association will be held in Princeton, New Jersey, at the Frontier Inn, on January 19, 19XX, at 7:30 P.M. If you will be unable to attend, please sign this stamped, self-addressed proxy card and return it promptly.

PROXY

I hereby constitute David Jordan, Marilee Addington, and Louis Pradella, who are officers or directors of the Association, or a majority of such of them as actually are present, to act for

me in my stead and as my proxy at the January meeting of the Business Association, to be held in Princeton, New Jersey, at the Frontier Inn, on January 19, 19XX, at 7:30 P.M., and at any adjournment or adjournments thereof, with full power and authority to act for me in my behalf, with all powers that I, the undersigned, would possess if I were personally present.

Effective Date:_____

Signed:_____

City_____State_____Zip Code_____

PLEASE BE CERTAIN TO COMPLETE THE ABOVE FORM IN FULL BEFORE MAILING. NO POSTAGE IS REQUIRED.

Proxies are important when it's likely that not enough members will be present at the meeting to constitute the quorum required to transact business. The notice and proxy form do not have to be combined, however; follow the preferred practice in your organization or any requirements stated in the bylaws (use announcements of previous meetings as a guide). Perhaps your organization always encloses a check-off attendance reply card: "I will ( ) will not ( ) attend the January 19, 19XX, meeting of the Business Association." The member would fill in his or her name and address and check the appropriate place for designating intentions. This type of reply card can be especially useful if you're holding a lunch or dinner meeting and you need to know in advance how many meals to order (state on the reply card a deadline for returning it).

Like the notice, the agenda for the meeting should be prepared according to the format required by or preferred by your organization (study examples from previous meetings). Sometimes the meeting chair or secretary solicits items for the agenda before preparing it. A board of directors, for instance, that meets infrequently might want to be certain it doesn't forget anything and that everyone has an opportunity to add matters of importance to the agenda. In such a case, you could write to the members of the board, stating that you're preparing the agenda and if anyone has anything to be included he or she should send it to you by a certain date. For events such as board meetings, your organization also might distribute advance copies of the agenda so that everyone can study the topics and be prepared to act on the items—sometimes it's very important to give people a chance to do their homework before coming to the meeting. In any case, begin preparing the agenda early, in sufficient time for an exchange of correspondence with others before the meeting. Some people start preparing the agenda for the next meeting the day after the previous meeting has ended. A computer is helpful when you will be making numerous additions and changes in the agenda, since you can make your revisions easily and print out an up-to-date copy at any time.

Which items you should put on the agenda will depend on the type of meeting and its objectives. If it's time to elect new officers, that item will be prominent on the agenda; otherwise, it will be omitted. Study the bylaws carefully to determine any requirements that would affect the topics listed and the format, general preparation, and distribution of the agenda. If any members are coming from out of town, you may want to enclose a map with directions marked to the site, as well as recommendations for transportation or overnight accommodations. The agenda might have some or all of these topics (or additional topics, depending on the particular meeting):

AGENDA

Business Association
January 19, 19XX, 7:30 P.M.
Frontier Inn
Princeton, N.J. 08540

Call to order
Reading, correction, and approval of previous minutes

Officers' reports
Executive committee report
Standing committees' reports
Special committees' reports
Unfinished business
New business
Announcements
Adjournment

But both the preliminary and the final agenda will contain more detailed listings. Under "officers' reports," for instance, you might list "treasurer," "first vice-president," or any other officer who will be reporting. Under "unfinished business," you would list matters pending from an earlier meeting. Under "new business" you would list matters to be considered that were not discussed previously. Additionally, the presiding officer should have a file with even more detailed information concerning each item. All members, in fact, may want to prepare notes or a meeting folder with printed reports and any other data they might need to refer to in order to comment or vote on the various agenda items. (For details about the conduct of the meeting and the transaction of business, see "Officers and Committees" [Article X] and "Introduction of Business" [Article XI] in the rules portion of this book.)

Publicity and Promotion

Some meetings require extensive promotion and need as much publicity as possible to ensure success; for others, publicity and promotion would be inappropriate. You wouldn't hold a press conference or do a mass mailing to announce the regular Monday morning meeting of your office staff or the quarterly meeting of the First Lutheran Church Board of Directors. But any meeting that relies on the participation of the general public or interested outside persons has to be announced to the prospective audience in some way (see also the preceding section, "Meeting Notices and Agendas"). It needs more than a simple announcement, in fact; it needs strategic publicity and promotion to ensure adequate attendance.

Organizations that hold large meetings such as a trade show or conference usually have a separate promotion or publicity and promotion committee. In some cases, the Program Committee (see "Program Development" in the first chapter) handles publicity and promotion; in other cases, when the meeting is not particularly complex, one person alone may be appointed to handle this part of the meeting arrangements. But assume again that you're a member of a national organization and are involved in arranging a large, three-day meeting in Cleveland; the Planning Committee has just appointed you to serve as the chair of the Publicity and Promotion Committee— where do you start?

Your first step will be to select one to three persons to serve on your committee and to call a meeting of the committee as soon as possible. Brief yourself, however, before you attempt to brief your committee members. This means that you should review any instructions you received from the Planning Committee, read the bylaws and any other rules of your organization that might affect your activity, and meet with other key organizers such as the meeting chair, the meeting coordinator, and the finance chair. The finance chair will no doubt ask you to submit a proposed budget for your committee and, upon approval, will let you know how much you may spend, for which items you'll need prior authorization, and so on. (Review the preliminary steps for a committee described in "Finance" in the first chapter.)

During your first committee meeting, give the members an address list of the other committees and provide any information you have on the meeting's theme, objectives, and desired audience. Explain what previous promotion committees did and outline the activities you expect to pursue for the Cleveland meeting. Provide the members with a schedule and suggested deadlines. (The members may have useful suggestions about all of this and other matters.)

Assign tasks to your committee members. One person might be in charge of securing quotes and schedules from printers for any literature to be printed (such as an early announcement, the main premeeting program-registration packet, and an on-site program booklet). Someone else might look into sources of mailing lists (does your organization maintain its own lists or do you have to buy or rent outside lists?) and services for addressing and mailing. This person should secure quotes and the required timetable for any mailings and determine bulk-rate and other postal costs and requirements (does your organization have or should it obtain a bulk-rate permit?). Perhaps you'll assign yourself the task of exploring the various outside promotional options (an airline, for example, sometimes will do a promotional mailing for an organization if it is declared the "official" airline for the meeting). Or you may want to retain a public-relations company or an advertising firm to prepare any promotional packages you need and to arrange for the mailings; the news releases, radio announcements, and television spots; and any premeeting or on-site press conferences.

All of these things cost money, however, so all of the committee members should get several quotes for items such as printing and mailing and submit them to you. Budget limitations may force you to rule out using outside services such as a public relations or advertising firm. In that case, you'll have to work with a printer yourself, write your own press releases, and prepare any other promotional material that you need. Presumably, however, you and the other committee members will have a personal office staff to help you do routine tasks such as proofreading material from the printer and preparing press releases and other copy for mailing. But you and your committee members will have to plan everything—develop the strategies; prepare a schedule for program printing and mailing, press-release mailings, and other types of publicity and promotion that you decide to use; supervise the entire operation; and coordinate your committee's work with other key players such as the program chair, the finance chair, and the person in charge of advance and on-site registration. (If there's a meeting coordinator, your task in regard to contact with other committees should be a lot easier.)

The Program Committee will probably give you a typed or computer-prepared draft of the three-day program, and the Registration Committee (or the person on the Program Committee in charge of registration details) should provide copy for the registration instructions and the card or form that registrants are supposed to fill out and return with their registration fees. These committees or other persons should give you information about other matters—hotel accommodations, transportation to and from the airports, a site map, entertainment for participants and spouses, day-care facilities in the hotel, accommodations for the handicapped, publications and other items to be sold at the meeting, and special features or unusual events. If the Program Committee hasn't organized this mix of information, your task will be to put it in order for the proposed brochure or other conference mailer, to edit it to size so that the packet to be mailed won't be too large for your printing and postage budget, and to work with the printer on all of this. If you retain a public relations or advertising firm to handle such matters, however, someone else will take care of these details. Either way, the schedule should clearly take into account the time required for a third-class (bulk-rate) package to reach prospects and the time they need to get company authorization to attend the event and send in their registration fees. (Ask your local post office about the time required for mailing at the third-class rate or other rates.) Work closely in regard to schedules with the Program Committee and the Registration Committee—you can't get anything printed and mailed until they give you the copy—and be certain that they know the deadlines that are involved. Once you have everything put together, submit it all to the Planning Committee for approval.

If you plan to advertise in magazines or trade journals and newspapers as well as on the radio or over television (paid advertising, that is), you will no doubt retain an advertising agency to create and place the ads for you. But you may write your own press releases to announce the upcoming meeting. Stick to the essential facts for this—time, date, and place; type of meeting, such as a technical conference; important features including prominent speakers; and other essential data.

Follow the examples of press releases used for earlier meetings. Does your organization have a press-release letterhead? Otherwise, use the organization's regular business letterhead. Observe the key elements of an effective release (one that will get printed). Use a typewriter or a computer and make additional copies by computer, mimeograph, photocopier, or any such means, but don't send carbon copies. If your organization doesn't have a press list, use one of the directories such as *Ayer's* (found in a library reference room) and compile a suitable list. Double-space all pages (type —*more*— at the end of each page to be continued), but keep the release as succinct as possible—and put the paragraphs in order of importance; editors cut from the bottom up. If you have ten paragraphs, for example, an editor may delete the last eight and keep the first two. At the top right, just below the printed letterhead, identify someone the press can contact in your organization:

For further information:
John Jones, 602-673-1004

Add an address for John Jones if it's different from the letterhead address. A couple of inches down, center the date you are releasing the information (usually "immediately"):

FOR IMMEDIATE RELEASE

The press prefers to write its own headlines, so you can omit that. Begin your first paragraph with a dateline:

DETROIT, MICH., March 11, 19XX: The twenty-sixth annual meeting and technical conference of the . . .

Use straightforward language—no sensational adjectives such as *tremendous* or *amazing*. A photograph may be enclosed, if appropriate (perhaps a revolutionary product will be unveiled at the meeting); send an 8 ½- by 10-inch black and white glossy and at the end of the release write "Photograph Enclosed." On the last page of the release at the bottom write "—30—" or "END." Use printed second sheets for additional pages or a plain sheet of paper with the page number at the top right and a word or two summarizing the subject of the release at the top left. Although you may be mailing to numerous journals and newspapers, all with different deadlines for the next issue, keep in mind that a release must reach a publication by its stated deadline for accepting material in order to appear in the next issue or edition.

Depending on your meeting—size, type, and objective— you may do more or less than suggested here to get the word out before the meeting and to secure publicity for your organization during and after the conference as well. You might, for example, notify the editors of journals and newspapers that a press conference will be held during the meeting to make a special announcement or introduce a prominent speaker (it will have to be important to get the press out). After the meeting you may send another release to announce important things that happened during the meeting or to announce the availability of published proceedings. On the other hand, you may not have the budget or need for the publicity and promotional options described here. Perhaps your meeting has an audience almost guaranteed to attend and meeting-room limitations such that you don't want to encourage greater attendance. Every meeting is different, and you will have to tailor your publicity and promotion to fit your own special requirements. In any case, you should conclude your activities for the meeting by writing a final Publicity and Promotion Committee report and submitting it to the Planning Committee. (For more about the program-registration package, see "Program Development" in the first chapter, "Registration" in this chapter, and "Proceedings" in the fourth chapter.)

Registration

Meetings such as seminars and conferences have two types of registration for participants—preregistration, or advance registration, and on-site, or door, registration. A prime objective of any registration committee is to get as many people as possible registered—with fees paid—in advance. A seminar or workshop with established limits on attendance (perhaps registration closes after the first forty registrations) doesn't have the same concerns as a conference that's open to as many people as the sponsor can entice to come. In the latter case, just about everything hinges on numbers. How many meeting rooms and meals should be ordered—enough for five hundred, a thousand, two thousand? How much should be charged for registration? Presumably, the fee could be, and would be, less if attendance were two thousand than if it were two hundred.

To make intelligent decisions about reservations and financial matters, one has to have a fairly accurate estimate of attendance. To a certain extent, this estimate is made in the early planning stages based on experience (previous meeting attendance) and projected response to promotional activity. But firm figures are possible only with hard evidence—the receipt of actual registration forms and checks. Although large conferences nearly always have some on-site, or door, registration, it could be overwhelming to have hundreds of people unexpectedly appear at the door on the opening day of the meeting: Would it still be possible to get additional meeting rooms or larger rooms? Could the hotel suddenly feed, say, four hundred unexpected attendees? Could a printer quickly provide that many extra programs? (One always does an overrun, however, in case more people show up later.) On reflection, it becomes clear that an organization should strive to get most people registered well in advance of the meeting date.

Consider again the example used in previous sections: a national organization holding a three-day meeting in Cleveland. This time you're chair of the Registration

Committee—what are your duties? First, review the description of preliminary steps provided in "Finance" in the first chapter: Select one to three people to be on your committee, set a date for the first meeting, and prepare for it by studying the bylaws and other rules, previous meeting materials, and instructions from the Planning Committee.

At the first committee meeting, give the members an address list of the other committees, review the meeting theme, objectives, desired audience and attendance, and other key elements. Be prepared to make committee task assignments. Perhaps one person will be in charge of creating the registration form and working with a printer (or with the person who is in charge of printing for the meeting); another might be in charge of processing incoming registrations; someone else might be responsible for setting up a booth at the conference site and arranging for assistants to operate it.

The finance chair will no doubt ask you for a Registration Committee budget right away and, upon its approval, will tell you what your committee may spend and which items require prior authorization. If the Publicity and Promotion Committee is arranging to print and mail a general program-registration package, your job will be to draft the portion pertaining to registration—copy to go in the instructional part of the packet concerning when and how to register and an actual card or sheet that people can fill out and mail in with their check. The program or publicity chair will then get approval of the package from the Planning Committee and will arrange for the mass mailing.

The registration fee must be set based on anticipated attendance and overall meeting expenses. A number of people will be involved in the decision-making process. Although the Planning Committee will authorize the final figure, you and the finance chair should be actively involved in this part of the meeting arrangements. Other committee chairs also have information that's important. The facilities and meals chairs, for example, have cost figures that may influence the final decision.

Perhaps the decision will be to have a varied fee structure, with a low general fee but extra charges for special events such as a dinner-dance and for a copy of the proceedings. Or you may have one fee that covers everything. Also, members of the organization may have a lower registration fee than the one for nonmembers. Late registrations (after a certain date or at the door) may be higher—to encourage people to register and pay early. Another question concerns the method of payment—will you allow credit cards? Will you accept unpaid registrations and bill people? Will you refund 100 percent on cancellation up to a certain date and less after that date? Will you give group discounts or student discounts? (Note that your organization may have a strict policy about some of these matters.) Once the Planning Committee, with recommendations from you and the finance chair, has decided these matters, you can incorporate the information into your draft for the program-registration packet.

You need to have efficient procedures for tallying registrations as they arrive (how many are registered for this or that session, how many in all?) and sending updated reports to the Program Committee and the Planning Committee. If there's a meeting coordinator, this person will keep the other key players informed. Nearly everyone will be watching registration returns closely. The finance chair will want to know how income and expenses are running. The Facilities Committee and the Meals and Entertainment Committee will want to know if they've underbooked or overbooked. The Program Committee will be wondering if it needs to add more sessions to accommodate excessive attendance or cancel some if attendance is running below estimates. Because so much hinges on attendance, you need to have accurate records and be able to report changes regularly (daily, in some instances). Have your staff keep a tally sheet as the mail is opened each day.

Although you will likely keep the actual incoming registration forms in an alphabetical file (where new ones can be added and cancellations pulled out), it would be too time consuming to have someone recount the forms every day—hence the need for continually updated tally sheets. But you also may want to enter everything into a computer, maintaining a registrant address list with data such as amount paid, sessions selected, and tickets purchased for special events. This list could be updated right up to the time of leaving for the conference and could be used at the on-site registration desk as a check-in guide. Finally, in regard to records, coordinate your registration-processing activities with the accounting department and the bookkeeper in charge of recording income and expenses. You'll have to turn over receipts to the designated person along with names or other information as requested.

By the time forms and checks begin to arrive, you should have an office staff set up and trained to do the paperwork and answer telephone inquiries. You will have to decide whether to transport this staff to the meeting site to run the registration desk there or whether the staff is needed at the home site during the meeting. If the staff won't be going, you'll need to arrange (through the hotel or a convention bureau) for secretarial services or an outside staff to take over during the meeting—or you may use volunteers from among the membership of your organization.

Some things can be secured on site through the hotel (such as copying facilities and typewriters), but most supplies you'll need to transport to the site. Make a list of supplies and records that should be taken to the meeting site and find out what materials other committees will be sending for use or distribution at the registration desk. Your list should include these items:

- Typewriters or portable computers

- Diskettes

- Files

- Cash lockboxes (arrange to take cash receipts to a bank—don't leave a lot of cash laying around—and put it in a hotel safe if the banks are closed)

- Credit-card machines

- Notebooks

- Pens and pencils
- Receipt books
- Badges for registrants (the badges can be typed at the home office as registrations come in; have them in alphabetical order at the on-site registration desk)
- Maps and brochures of the city
- Tickets to special events
- Signs

Some things may be mailed in advance to people who register early. At any rate, as registration forms arrive, you should immediately mail a confirmation notice to registrants. (This may be a printed card or duplicate copy of the registration form marked "paid"—study the confirmation notices used at previous meetings, or ask your printer to show you samples of such notices and other registration materials.)

The hotel will provide a table or booth for the registration staff. Let the Facilities Committee know what your needs will be and where you want the booth located. Often the registration desk or booth is in a prominent location in a lobby or hallway where attendees will see it immediately on arriving at the portion of the hotel set aside for the meeting. (But be certain it doesn't complicate the traffic flow to meeting rooms.) If a table is used, arrange for floor-length skirts so that you can store supplies beneath it, out of sight. Put signs on poles or in some other visible place to specify things such as "Advance Registration Check-In" and "New Registrations," "Name Tags," "Ticket Sales," "Proceedings Sales," and "Press Kits." In the same area, other committees may set up their own booths, such as a child-care check-in desk or an information booth. All of this activity should be arranged through or coordinated with the Facilities Committee.

Have strategies prepared for dealing with troublesome registrants. Although attendance etiquette requires that registrants be quiet, courteous, and cooperative at a meeting, not everyone has the best possible manners. You may find unruly people—some who are angry that the session they wanted to attend is full, and even thieves. It's not unusual to find that copies of proceedings on sale have disappeared or even cash boxes that are suddenly gone without a trace. The Planning Committee may appoint someone to remove unruly people (see Section 67 in the rules portion of the book on the right of an organized assembly to eject someone). Otherwise, decide in advance (with the Facilities Committee and the meeting chair) who will handle such problems. In regard to theft, be prepared with good security—don't hesitate to have a staff member or volunteer from the organization act as a watchdog in the registration area. Establish advance procedures with the hotel security staff (the Facilities Committee may do this) so that you know the person to call if a crime occurs; keep a number for the local police handy as well. Also, have a place for people to report lost and found items (the hotel will also have such a department). Finally, find out from the Facilities Committee if there's a house physician or someone else to contact if illness or injury is reported at the registration desk.

Arrange to return all records and supplies to the home site after the meeting. Make your final accounting to the bookkeeper or accounting department (although you still may have to bill some unpaid registrations when you return). When the last registration fee or other receipt is accounted for and your registration list for the meeting is complete, make a final report to the Planning Committee.

Facilities

Site and Facilities Arrangements

AN ORGANIZATION sometimes has a circuit it travels for meetings. Perhaps a significant percentage of its membership or other interested people is located in various large cities such as Chicago or Los Angeles. It's almost a necessity, then, to schedule meetings in each of the cities with such large clusters of prospective attendees. Other organizations may simply choose a city that will appeal to people for other reasons: It may be a wonderful place to visit or an ideal place to which to bring the family for a combined meeting and vacation. The choice of the particular facilities (such as a hotel or convention center) is not always as obvious. A lot can go wrong, in fact, with this part of the meeting arrangements.

Once again, assume that you're one of the key arrangers of a national organization holding a three-day meeting in Cleveland—a substantial portion of the organization's membership and prospective audience is there, and the organization hasn't met in Cleveland for five years, so it's time to return. Your assignment for this meeting is to chair the Facilities Committee. Specifically, you will be concerned with selecting the best hotel, convention center, university, town hall, or other place to hold the three-day event. After the facility is chosen, you'll be concerned with details such as how many rooms are needed, what size they should be, and what they will cost.

The Planning Committee may have indicated its facilities preference for the meeting but may want you to make other suggestions. Your first task, then, is to form a committee and set a date for a meeting. Follow the preliminary steps given in "Finance" in the first chapter: Review the bylaws and rules of the organization, find out what the Planning Committee wants, and prepare a committee address list and summary of key meeting objectives to give to your committee members. Have a preliminary meeting schedule prepared and be certain that the committee members know the various deadlines. Check whether there are any forms from previous meetings that you can use (supplies checklist, for example) or devise your own.

Assign tasks to your committee members at this first meeting. Initially, everyone may be assigned one or more facilities in the city to investigate (to visit, collect literature about, and determine general suitability). After that, one person may be in charge of arrangements for the meeting rooms, someone else may handle the rooms for meals or entertainment, and another person may see about airport transportation to the hotel for out-of-town visitors.

But initially, make a list of things you want each committee member to find out concerning the prospective facilities. Since the appropriate facilities should be visited in person (a telephone call or letter won't do for serious possibilities), it will help to have local residents on the committee. Once you have a list of things your organization will need from a facility, adjourn to meet (as soon as possible) again with enough information to select the best facility of the lot. Then submit your recommendation to the Planning Committee for final approval.

Your committee may have concluded after a thorough investigation of potential facilities that the New Hotel downtown has the most appropriate facilities for your meeting, and the Planning Committee agrees:

• Its prices are competitive.

• It has a reputation for excellent service.

- It's a modern facility and the location downtown is appealing, especially for attendees who bring along their spouses and children.

- There'll be plenty of parking in a new parking lot and more than adequate blocks of sleeping rooms.

- The meeting-room layouts, lighting, temperature, and furniture are perfect.

- The hotel has ramps, elevators, and other features to accommodate handicapped persons.

- It has a good paging system, active lost and found department, and clear directional signs.

- You have good reason to believe that the hotel staff will be very cooperative and will give your organization an abundance of assistance while you're making the arrangements and will help to ensure that all goes smoothly during the meeting.

Everyone agrees that it's an excellent choice, but this doesn't mean that you can relax. A facilities committee usually has an exceptionally heavy work load, and this is only the beginning for you and your committee members.

The finance chair will likely be waiting for a committee budget from you, and you should be able to prepare one fairly soon. The Program Committee will need details about the facilities to put in its program packet, and other committees also will be waiting for facilities information. The hotel, meanwhile, will have named a representative to work with you not only in selecting the physical accommodations but in establishing the related costs. But don't accept the first prices that are mentioned for the various facilities and services you need. Find out the usual rates for the things you need and negotiate the best price for your organization. If this is the first meeting of your organization at this hotel, you may have to make a deposit (the final bill will be payable after the event); arrange to make the deposit after a certain percentage of paid registrations has arrived. If your organization has met at this hotel before and has established credit with the hotel, the payment schedule may be more flexible. Nevertheless, it's common for hotels to ask for certain commitments concerning attendance; be prepared, therefore, to guarantee in writing the number of participants for certain events. If your attendance falls short, you still have to pay the agreed-upon amount. (Work with the Planning Committee and the Registration Committee in evaluating expected attendance.)

Hotels have their own contracts or agreements, but your organization also may have its own contracts for services at a facility (the hotel may insist on using its own, however). Either way, read the contract(s) carefully and be certain that everything you expect to receive is listed. This should include not only the service but the associated costs and a clarification of things the hotel will do and things your organization will do, as well as the deadlines or times that these things will be provided; do not use a facility that refuses to state all of such things in the contract. If something isn't specified, you may not get it later or at least not at the price you expected. Once you're satisfied, give a copy of the agreement(s) to the Planning Committee for it to study (the meeting chair usually signs contracts for the meeting).

By now you no doubt have submitted a facilities budget to the finance chair and have received approval, with an indication of what you may spend or contract for on your own, without prior authorization, and what must first be approved. It's time, then, to move immediately toward establishing the supplies and accommodations that you'll need. (You'll also need some of this information in order to determine what to have listed on the contract.) Ask each committee to send you a detailed list of its requirements (a meeting coordinator is very helpful in making such contacts with other committees) and ask the Program Committee to send you a list of speaker requirements. Also request a list from the Registration Committee or any other person or committee that needs rooms, supplies, equipment, or anything else at the meeting.

Depending on the complexity of the meeting, you could handle the detailed arrangements in various ways. But in all meetings, it's important to have separate lists of requirements for items such as the following:

- Supplies (including working supplies for the staff and speakers)
- Rooms (registration, meeting, sleeping, eating, entertaining)
- Meals and refreshments
- Social events
- Exhibits and displays
- Equipment for speakers
- Wheelchairs and other aids for handicapped attendees
- On-site secretarial, registration, and other personnel
- Signs
- Transportation (of materials and of participants and speakers to and from airports or other locations)

The hotel representative will need a copy of each list, as will the Planning Committee and the meeting coordinator; each committee will need a copy of the list pertaining to its own function.

By now you will have written instructions from the hotel concerning what you may and may not do. This will affect where you set up booths, where you sell publications and other items, where you put up signs, and so on. You will also soon know which items on your various lists you must provide and which the hotel will provide. Make new lists of the supplies, equipment, personnel, and other things that you must provide and contact the appropriate people in your organization to determine what's in stock and what must be ordered; place any necessary orders and reservations immediately.

Begin working on the physical layout and room-setup requirements. The Program Committee can give you a schedule of speakers and room-setup requirements for each one, including handout material, equipment, and supplies. Make committee and on-site staff assignments to handle the arrival and distribution of the various materials and equipment at the appropriate times. Be certain that reservations for materials and other orders have all been placed and check before the meeting to ensure that everything has arrived or will be arriving on time. Arrange for the transportation of any materials that won't be delivered by a supplier to the hotel. (See "Equipment and Presentation Aids" and "Exhibits and Demonstrations" in this chapter.)

Although a large committee or staff can be unwieldy without strong supervision and coordination, there's so much to do with facilities arrangements that it helps to have enough assistants available so that no one is overwhelmed with too much work. It's sometimes easier if one person can focus exclusively on one or a few related things such as supplies, equipment, and presentation aids for speakers; someone else might be concerned exclusively with transportation needs; another person might handle room setup (such as theater style, with everyone facing the front; classroom style, with rectangular tables and people facing the front; or conference-banquet style, with round or horseshoe tables and people facing each other); other assistants would similarly handle other tasks. Throughout all of this, maintain open communications with the meeting coordinator and other committees such as the Registration Committee and the Meals and Entertainment Committee. Their needs may change, and you in turn may have to make adjustments in your facilities arrangements (be certain to notify the finance chair immediately if your budget must be revised).

At the site, during the meeting, maintain an ongoing check of the facilities, supplies, and other items and see that the various people assigned to the different tasks monitor their activities properly throughout the meeting and afterward. Even after the meeting has ended, there are numerous tasks still to be handled. All of the things that were ordered and transported to the site have to be returned, bills have to be reviewed and forwarded for payment, and a detailed concluding report must be prepared for the Planning Committee.

Meals and Entertainment

Many organizations serve lunch, dinner, or morning or afternoon refreshments (or all of these things) during a meeting. Sometimes such meetings are held in a company conference room and the participants adjourn to the company dining room for the meal. Or snacks and beverages may be catered to the meeting room in the morning or afternoon. But many meetings are held in a hotel or motel, sometimes near a major airport if some of the participants come from out of town. In that case, one usually selects a menu and arranges with the facility to seat a certain number during the meal; often the food and beverages are brought into the meeting room by the hotel or motel catering service or restaurant personnel. The arrangements for meals and snacks become more complicated, though, when you're planning for a longer meeting, particularly one that runs two or more days.

The Facilities Committee might handle food and beverage arrangements, but sometimes there is a separate meals or meals and entertainment committee. Assume that you're the chair of such a committee for a national organization preparing to hold a three-day meeting in Cleveland. Like all of the other chairs, you'll start by reviewing instructions from the Planning Committee, preliminary information about the proposed meeting, and the organization's bylaws and other rules. You'll then select one to three people to serve on your committee and set up a first meeting. At this meeting you'll want to explain the purpose and objectives of the three-day event and brief your committee members on instructions, organization policy, deadlines, and the procedure followed by previous meals and entertainment committees. You should also give everyone an address list of the other committees and make work assignments. Finally, before adjourning, you should set a date for the next committee meeting. (See "Finance" in the first chapter for an outline of preliminary committee procedures.)

The Finance Committee will need a meals and entertainment budget from you as soon as possible and, after it has been approved, will let you know what you may spend on your own and what will require prior authorization. Other committees also will be waiting for information from you. The Registration Committee, for instance, has to consider meals and entertainment details in writing copy for the registration form and for any tickets to be used for special functions; the cost of food and beverages as well as entertainment also figures in the price of registration for the meeting. The Program Committee needs details on food and beverages and on entertainment to add to the instructions that will be part of the program-registration mailer, and it needs to list any cocktail party, banquet, or other special event on the program.

Depending on your organization and the type of meeting, the Planning Committee may instruct you concerning how many meals are desired and what kind of entertainment is desired, or you may be asked to recommend such things and provide the schedule. Either way, you'll be working closely with the Planning Committee and the Facilities Committee, as well as other committees. (A meeting coordinator will be very helpful in maintaining open communication with all of the key arrangers.)

In regard to the major meals, assume that everyone wants to provide—as part of the registration fee—three lunches, one dinner, and one cocktail party (preceding dinner), with a small musical group or perhaps just a piano player. Members and their families may, in addition, purchase tickets for a tour of the cultural sites in the city (perhaps one tour each afternoon). How do you arrange all of this? Contact the hotel representative assigned to work with the Facilities Committee (he or she may contact you) and arrange a meeting, preferably with the facilities chair present since meals also require rooms—the responsibility of the Facilities Committee. Explain to the hotel representative what your organization wants and ask what the hotel has to offer to accommodate those needs.

The hotel will want you to give an attendance guarantee on all meals probably forty-eight hours in advance of each event. You then have to pay for the number you guarantee, even if fewer registrants appear. A hotel can usually accommodate up to 10 percent more than your estimate, and you should ask the Facilities Committee to arrange for rooms of adequate size in case attendance increases unexpectedly at the last minute. (The meeting chair usually signs all contracts including any for meals and entertainment; be certain to submit your meals and entertainment plans and schedule to the Planning Committee for approval.) Also, discuss with the Facilities Committee the type of room settings (such as banquet style) and lighting that are needed for the particular meal or event.

Selecting the menus for the three lunches and the one dinner should be a joint activity. Let the hotel representative know that you'd like to see a choice of menus and listen to the advice of others on your own committee and on the Facilities Committee. Perhaps someone can point out ethnic or other considerations in the choice of foods and beverages. In general, lunches should be lighter than dinners, and the meat should be different for each meal—attendees would grow weary of chicken every day. Avoid the "vegetable of the day" type of menu, since then you don't know what you're getting until the meal. Alcohol is not recommended—registrants want to stay awake during the sessions—although a cocktail party or cash bar is common before a dinner (it closes, then, in one to two hours), provided it also serves nonalcoholic beverages. Also, keep in mind that exotic meals involving a lot of distraction while being served are a poor choice when there's going to be a guest lunch or dinner speaker.

Your organization may decide to provide morning and afternoon refreshment breaks in addition to the meals. Refreshment breaks, which may be set up in meeting rooms or in hallways (if they don't interrupt traffic flow), or the registration lobby, usually consist of coffee and other beverages such as fruit juice or soft drinks. Snacks may include donuts, rolls, cookies, granola bars, or sherbert. Although some groups try to economize by skipping breaks, this is usually counterproductive; most attendees need to refresh themselves to avoid attention loss and fatigue during the many sessions they attend throughout the day.

Decide what other meals you want to offer (such as breakfast for a board of directors meeting) and then look at the prices for the various meals and refreshment breaks. Ask the hotel representative to clarify costs—do the prices include gratuities and taxes? If everything is more than your budget can accommodate, ask the hotel representative to suggest subtle economies (during breaks, for example, a glass full of a chilled beverage alone costs more than a glass that's half beverage and half crushed ice). Once you have menus that you like and prices that you can afford, be certain that it's all guaranteed in the contract—don't take a chance that prices will be the same by the time the meeting arrives.

Tickets are usually printed for special events, such as a banquet or tour, especially when the price is not included in the registration fee. Often, if music or other entertainment is to be provided at a cocktail party or one of the meals, arrangements can be made through the hotel. But organizations also may contract on their own with outside musicians (consistent with hotel regulations for entertainment on the premises). Tours, too, are commonly arranged through the hotel, and large facilities regularly help visitors secure theater tickets, passes to sporting events, and entry to other special events, whether or not they're part of the meeting program. The advance-registration material should announce special events and provide a place for registrants to make reservations. Tickets also are commonly sold in the registration area. If no more space is available for a particular event, a "sold out" notice should be posted and alternatives suggested for interested persons. Coordinate all of these arrangements closely with the Registration Committee, the Program Committee, and the Facilities Committee. In addition, report arrangements regularly to the Planning Committee.

During the meeting, monitor attendance carefully so that you know if your estimates for the meal are correct. Other members of your committee should participate in all of these matters. You may, in fact, designate one person to be in charge of lunches, another dinner and the refreshment breaks, and someone else the special events such as tours. Inform the finance chair immediately if the numbers—and costs—change at any time before or during the meeting.

After the meeting, make your final contact with the hotel representative, review all food, beverage, and entertainment bills for accuracy, and forward the bills to the designated person for approval and payment. Then submit a final report on the meals and entertainment function to the Planning Committee.

Equipment and Presentation Aids

Someone addressing a local club at lunch might talk for twenty-five minutes without using any equipment or other presentation aids except for a podium and a microphone. But a speaker at a seminar or conference would likely want at least a board such as a chalkboard and a pointer and possibly some type of slide, sound, or other projector. The task for the people in charge of this—often the Facilities and Program committees—is to find out what a speaker needs for his or her presentation and to order it and have it set up in the room where the person will be speaking. (See "Program Development" and "Speakers" in the first chapter and "Site and Facilities Arrangements" in this chapter.)

The Program Committee makes the first contact with a speaker and therefore is the logical committee to determine what equipment and presentation aids the speaker needs. A common procedure is to enclose an equipment checklist with each speaker's confirmation letter (the letter sent after someone accepts an invitation to speak). The speaker can then check each item on the checklist that he or she wants and return the list to the program chair (the person who writes the confirmation letter).

With a large meeting, such as the three-day meeting in Cleveland described in previous sections, the arrangements for equipment and presentation aids can be extensive. There could be thirty or more speakers, all wanting different equipment and presentation aids set up at different times in different rooms. Not only is there a lot of ordering to do, but the Facilities Committee must also see that the items are delivered to the site and set up—in proper working order—in the rooms before the speaker and audience arrive. Sometimes equipment must be changed in the brief period between sessions as one group is exiting and before the next group enters.

Some of the equipment and presentation aids will be available through the hotel; some your organization may have in stock; other items will have to be ordered from suppliers at the site (the hotel or local residents on the Facilities Committee can probably suggest places to contact). Anything the hotel can provide that's suitable and for which the rental charge is within your budget should be considered simply because it's either already at the site (which means you can avoid potential transportation problems and outside delivery complications) or the hotel takes care of the ordering and follow-up as well as delivery—for a price (but you should monitor everything anyway). If the hotel's charge for taking care of this is too high and you want to order from outside suppliers yourself, be certain to check whether the hotel will allow you to bring in the equipment in question. Regardless of your decision, anything the hotel is going to provide and the cost should be listed in the written contract. Some things are usually provided free by the hotel, however, such as chalkboards, erasers, and podiums—ask the hotel representative what is free and what must be rented. The contract should specify "no charge" for the free items.

Your organization may have a standard checklist for equipment and presentation aids. If it doesn't, prepare one that lists everything a speaker might need for your particular meeting.

- Projectors are common at large meetings, and a variety are available: overhead, 16mm and 8mm sound, filmstrip, 35mm slide (manual and carousel), and rear screen. Screens (which the hotel may provide free) are also needed when projectors are used.

- Sound is always a consideration. You'll need floor, lectern, clip-on, and other microphones; a PA system; recorders (such as cassette) and blank tapes; sound mixers; and so on. Ask the hotel for suggestions if your organization doesn't have a list that was already developed for previous meetings.

- Video equipment (usually expensive) might be requested by some speakers. Ask the hotel or a supplier for a list of accessory equipment used with a video presentation.

- Various boards will be needed such as chalkboards, chartboards, and bulletin boards. You also may need easels and pads. Accessory supplies would include chalk (choose dustless), pointers, and marking pens. Electronic boards will print copies of the information on the board that can then be distributed to attendees in the audience.

- Consider lighting and other electrical needs. Is the light suitable for the presentation and for the audience? Where do you plug in all of the equipment? Will adapters be needed? How about remote control? The hotel should thoroughly brief your committee about such matters.

- Podiums, or lecterns, vary from standing units to tabletop models. The amplification system needed depends not only on the size of the room and its acoustics but also on the type of lectern the speaker wants. Will the speakers need gavels at the podiums?

Make your checklist as detailed as possible. But assuming that some speaker will probably want something you don't have on the list, add several "other" lines: "( ) Other _____." Sometimes a speaker prefers to bring his or her own equipment or presentation aids, so your checklist should include a place for the speaker to list such items (and check who pays for the rental).

Setting up equipment and presentation aids for numerous speakers (as well as setting up the rooms with tables,
pencils, pads, fresh water, and other things for the attendees) is too much of a task for one person. The Facilities
Committee, working with the Program Committee, should
divide the labor among the various committee members,
staff assistants, and volunteers from the organization sponsoring the meeting. Time is crucial in the actual setup
process, so workers should be thoroughly briefed and
given schedules broken down into minutes. (Be alert to
labor-union rules and regulations when hotel or other
outside services are used.)

Be prepared for emergencies. Although a piece of
equipment should be tested before the speaker uses it,
and it should not be assumed that everything is working
properly, the equipment still could fail during a presentation. What would you do? Have emergency strategies
written out for everyone, especially where backup equipment can be secured instantly (develop your backup strategies in cooperation with the hotel representative so
everyone clearly understands what can and should be
done in such an emergency).

After the meeting, collect and review all rental bills
and forward them to the appropriate person for payment. When the last task is finished, submit a final report
to the Planning Committee.

Exhibits and Demonstrations

Organizations whose members deal in products that can
be displayed or demonstrated at a meeting may want to
hold a trade show or incorporate exhibits into the program of a conference. A national organization holding a
three-day conference in Cleveland might want to allocate
some space for members and others to display and dem-
onstrate their products. Such displays might consist only
of printed material and photographs or they might include products and equipment. If the Planning Commit-

tee wants something more extensive than just a few booths with literature handouts, it should appoint an Exhibits Committee to handle these arrangements (or the Facilities Committee might handle them).

Assume that you've just been appointed exhibits chair. Follow the preliminary steps outlined in "Finance" in the first chapter: Review instructions from the Planning Committee, study the bylaws and other rules, and select one to three people for your committee. Set up a committee meeting as soon as possible and brief the members on the objectives, schedules, and other details of the upcoming meeting. Give each member an address list of other committees and describe procedures established by previous exhibits committees. Finally, make task assignments. Someone might work with the Facilities Committee in regard to space requirements (perhaps you want display areas of ten-by-ten feet each); another member might handle materials the exhibitors will need (tables, wall boards, and so on); someone else might be in charge of the physical installation, operation, and removal of the exhibits.

You will be busy, at least initially, in developing a list of prospective exhibitors (from former conferences, trade journals, membership directories, yellow pages, and other likely sources of prospects), preparing an exhibits budget for the finance chair (who will let you know what is approved and what expenditures you may incur with or without prior authorization), and developing exhibit and display rules and regulations with the Planning Committee (hours exhibits will be open, type of materials that will be allowed, type of demonstrations that will be allowed, rental fees for display space, and so on). Exhibitors should be selected that will enhance the overall meeting program; products and equipment displayed should be reliable and reputable (you wouldn't, for instance, want to allow someone to display a product on the verge of being banned as a health hazard).

You or the facilities chair will need to confirm with the hotel representative what may or may not be brought on the premises and what hotel charges will be involved for holding a show. Meanwhile, the Publicity and Promotion

Committee will be waiting for details from you to include in its publicity announcements, and the Program and Registration committees will need details for the advance program-registration mailer. (A meeting coordinator will be very helpful in maintaining the necessary contacts with other committees.) When details are firm, you should contact the prospective exhibitors.

The displays will have certain space, electrical, and other requirements. Often exhibits are set up in one or more rooms that can be divided by curtains or partitions into numerous individual areas. The hotel may offer this type of setup service, but even so, if its fee is too high, you may want to check the yellow pages for a firm that provides trade-show services at more reasonable cost. Some organizations will do everything—contact the prospective exhibitors, book the space, contract with the hotel, and, in general, run the entire show.

If you don't want the hotel or an outside firm to set up the show—or if your budget won't permit this—you will need a good team of volunteers to assist you. Develop a floor plan for the displays as soon as you know what space will be available in the hotel (if the show is going to be extremely large, you'll probably be meeting in a convention center with a huge showroom and specially designed places for exhibits). Draw a scale floor plan and number the individual exhibit areas—perhaps you plan to have fifty exhibits. Exhibitors, then, can be assigned numbered display areas when they want to reserve space. Include aisles and entry and exit doorways on your drawing so that you can visualize traffic flow.

The first letter to prospective exhibitors should make the following points:

- Introduce your organization

- Describe the upcoming meeting

- Profile the expected exhibits

- Provide a timetable or schedule for the displays

- Give the prospects a good reason for exhibiting their products or equipment

The letter should be accompanied by a reply card so that interested parties can ask for more information with minimal effort.

The next contact—a follow-up mailing to the best prospects, including those who sent back reply cards—should give more details about the exhibits:

- Enclose a copy of your floor plan.

- Provide details on rental charges for exhibit spaces.

- Give specific program information.

- State essential facts about the hotel.

- Provide information on security.

- Explain transportation and shipping requirements.

- Make a clear statement about the type of equipment and products that are desired for display.

- State delivery times and places.

- Enclose a copy of the contract that exhibitors must sign.

On the contract, have lines for the exhibitors to specify the type of display (with a list of associated equipment and supplies) they will have, any physical requirements (such as tables, chairs, or electrical needs), and the space desired (selected from your numbered floor plan), with second and third choices. If you'll be providing the signs, have a space on the contract for the exhibitors to specify the desired wording for their exhibit signs. If you're going to provide name tags apart from those prepared by the Registration Committee, ask the exhibitors to specify the names, job titles, and company affiliations for all who will need name tags at the exhibits. The Planning Committee may have a standard contract it uses for displays at its conferences or for separate trade shows; otherwise, if you draft the contract, submit it to the Planning Committee for approval (the meeting chair usually signs all contracts).

Assign on-site duties to members of your committee,

staff assistants, and volunteers from your organization. If you're not going to have the hotel or a trade-show service set up the display area, have your own crew briefed and ready to prepare the exhibit spaces before the conference opens. Assign some volunteers to welcome and register exhibitors and to welcome and direct viewers when the displays open. One or more persons should serve as contacts for the exhibitors (set up an information desk or the like for this purpose) with needs and problems. If labor unions are involved, tailor your procedures and activities to meet union requirements. See that strict security is observed during the meeting and be certain that exhibitors have a place to store money and other valuables during off hours.

Throughout the process of arranging for the exhibits and during the show, keep the Planning Committee informed. After the exhibits close, collect and review final bills, forwarding them to the designated person for payment. Prepare a list of registered exhibitors (for future meetings) and make a detailed final report to the Planning Committee.

Meeting Records

TWO COMMON TYPES of meeting records are the minutes and a book of published proceedings. Minutes represent the record of business transacted at a meeting (the minutes may or may not be published). A book of published proceedings usually consists of an edited version of the papers presented by speakers at a seminar, conference, or other similar meeting.

Minutes

The recording officer of an organization (known as the clerk or secretary) is the official minute taker in a formal assembly. (See Sections 41 and 51 in the rules portion of this book for proper recording procedure under the rules of parliamentary law.) In many small, informal meetings, however, someone else, such as an office secretary or an outside recorder, may do the actual note taking. In addition, tape recorders are commonly used as a backup (someone always should take notes in case a tape recorder fails). But regardless of who actually writes down the information and regardless of how informal a meeting may be, it's important to have accurate notes of what was said and agreed to by the participants. With the exception of casual office or social conversations, notes should always be typed or printed out by computer in an organized form.

The bylaws of an organization should indicate what is required in this area. In any case, if you're holding an

organized meeting (an assembly of persons gathering specifically to discuss and decide matters), someone should
record the information. The person doing the recording
should arrive before the meeting and assemble his or her
material and supplies (notebook, copy of agenda, forms
for recording motions and resolutions, reference material
on topics to be discussed or reported at the meeting,
pencils and pens, seating chart, and so forth). A recording secretary who is also an officer of the organization
should sit next to the chair. An office secretary or outside recorder would likely sit nearby in a position from
which it's possible to see all speakers during the meeting.
If you don't know everyone, make a seating chart so that
you can recognize speakers. If there are too many people
for this, ask the chair to direct people to identify themselves when they speak.

Even in a very formal meeting, the recorder usually
doesn't attempt to write down every single word that's
said. In most cases, the objective should be to record
essential facts (and to do so objectively) or the gist of
conversations:

**Messrs. Fontana and Sloane and Ms. Racemic
discussed the benefits of the new zoning law
for service industries.**

Resolutions, however, should be recorded in full, including the names of those who made or seconded a motion.
You might want to use a form for recording such material. In any case, record the following facts:

- Motion wording

- Motion made by

- Motion seconded by

- Number voting for

- Number voting against

A resolution normally begins with the word *RESOLVED*,
often followed by *That:*

RESOLVED That . . .

Write *WHEREAS* and *RESOLVED* in all capitals and use an initial capital for *That* when it follows *RESOLVED*. Capitalize *Board of Directors*, *Corporation*, and the like. Money should be written out with the numbers in parentheses afterward:

Two Hundred Dollars ($200.00)

If you're unsure about something, ask the chair or someone else about it during the next break in proceedings or just before you leave the meeting—definitely before you transcribe your notes. Also, note all times such as the time of the call to order or the adjournment and any other factual data concerning the order of business. You may have a copy of some material presented at the meeting, such as a treasurer's report. But take notes anyway; perhaps the copy has been revised and the treasurer is reporting new facts and figures at the meeting.

Transcribe your notes as soon as possible after the meeting while it's all still fresh in your mind. If you taped the activity, listen to the oral version and compare it with your written notes. Minutes are usually prepared by typewriter or computer and placed in a minute book along with copies of reports presented at the meeting. Use other prepared minutes of previous meetings as a guide to setup. If you can't find a sample to imitate, follow this procedure. Center the heading and include the name, type of meeting, and date:

The Fine Company
Board of Directors
Regular Monthly Directors Meeting
June 7, 19XX

In the first paragraph of the minutes, state the date, place, name of presiding officer, type of meeting, whether a quorum was present, and time the meeting was called to order. Use subheadings for individual topics in the body of the minutes (often you can use each item on the agenda as a separate heading). For a small meeting, list the names of attendees under the first paragraph:

CALL TO ORDER   **The regular monthly meeting of the Board of Directors of the Fine Company was called to order at 10:00 A.M., Monday, June 7, 19XX, in the Conference Room at 1276 First Avenue. The presiding officer was Wanda Musgrove. A quorum was present, including the following:**

[list alphabetically]

Absent were John Wyatt and Susan Moss.

If the minutes are brief, double-space the body and triple-space between each item; single-space resolutions. If they're very long, single-space them with a double space between paragraphs. When side subheadings are used (subheads also may be placed directly above each paragraph), it's not necessary to indent the paragraphs. Otherwise, indent them about ten spaces and indent all lines of a resolution about fifteen spaces. At the end—after the last paragraph, which is headed "Adjournment"—add two lines for the secretary (on the left) and the presiding officer (on the right) to write their signatures:

[handwritten signature]   [handwritten signature]
Secretary   **Chairman**

A minute book should be indexed so that subjects can be located quickly at any time, especially during future meetings. The index can be prepared by computer or typewriter. Typewritten indexes are commonly prepared on three-by-five-inch cards that can be alphabetized by topic. The information for each topic should include the subject and the date of the minutes and the book and page where the topic can be found. Every time the same subject comes up, add the new date and place beneath the previous one:

Zoning

> June 7, 19XX, Book 4, page 27
> September 5, 19XX, Book 4, page 51

A computer list might have the data arranged this way:

Zoning: June 7, 19XX, Book 4, page 27
September 5, 19XX, Book 4, page 51

The minutes may be corrected at future meetings, and the minute book has to be changed accordingly. On the typed or printed copy, draw a line in red ink through the incorrect words and write the correct words above them. In the margin next to the correction write the date of the meeting when the minutes were corrected (not the date you make the correction in the minute book). If the correction is large, cross out the incorrect copy as usual but add a separate page and, by the date notation in the margin, write a note to "see correction on page XXX" and insert the page at the end of the minutes for that meeting. On any such added page, include a signature line for the secretary and another for the chair, the same as you did at the bottom of the last page of the minutes, after the adjournment paragraph.

Proceedings

A paper presented by a speaker at a meeting such as a seminar or conference might be duplicated by the speaker and distributed to the attendees in the room. But some organizations like to publish a book containing all or most of the papers presented at the meeting. Such collections are commonly called *proceedings*. A free copy may be given to each registrant as part of the registration fee, or copies may be placed on sale at the meeting (sometimes organizations mail free copies to their members). Often the organization will print extra copies and during and after the meeting will promote and sell the books to try to recover some of the production costs, possibly earn a profit, and in any case at least fulfill its role of disseminating information to an interested public.

Assume that for the three-day meeting in Cleveland described in previous chapters you're in charge of the printed proceedings. Perhaps you're a member of the Program Committee, or perhaps the Planning Committee thinks that members of the Program Committee have enough to do and that a noncommittee member should be in charge of the proceedings. Either way, since the Program Committee is developing the program and selecting the speakers, it will no doubt also solicit written copies of each speaker's address. In that case, the papers that are collected will be turned over to you after the Program Committee has verified that they fulfill the requirements of the assigned topic and meet the specifications (length, style, and so on) initially provided by the committee to the speakers. (The committee may ask you to develop a set of manuscript-preparation instructions that can be photocopied and sent to each speaker.)

Collecting the papers would usually conclude the Program Committee's active role in the production of the book of proceedings if someone else has been assigned the task of supervising production. But you'll still want to maintain close contact with the committee in case there are changes in the program. It may be too late to put a late-arriving paper in the book, but you still may have to print the paper as a separate handout in addition to the book of proceedings.

If the Planning Committee didn't give you instructions concerning the type of proceedings desired and if there are no examples from previous years to use as a guide, ask the committee if it has any requirements before you contact printers for quotes. Some organizations want their proceedings to look like any other professionally produced bound book that you might see in a bookstore. Others prefer the most economical route, which might mean printing the papers exactly as they arrive from the speakers—errors and all—and either using them as individual handouts at the conference or assembling them together in some form such as in an inexpensive binder. This is also the easiest course for you, since you can't edit them if they're being used "as is," and therefore they won't need typesetting or proofreading—the speakers presumably will take care of such things before they submit their individual papers.

Assume, however, that your organization wants a much more polished product. It doesn't want to spend the money on a hardcover book—a paperback will do—but it does want each paper to be edited for consistency and to be typeset to look like a chapter in the book. The editing, proofreading, and the like are tasks that you can do on a volunteer basis, but after talking to the finance chair, you may have doubts about the organization being able to afford a handsome, but expensive, typeset product. The only way to find out what you can do, however, within the limits of the budget set by the Finance Committee (as approved by the Planning Committee), is to get quotes.

To simplify matters, since you don't have much time before the meeting, you probably would like to use a printer that can provide typesetting, printing, and binding as a package, rather than work with three separate firms (the printer, however, might subcontract with two other firms instead of doing everything on the premises). Select three such firms and get quotes on the project, but ask for separate figures on the typesetting, printing, and binding functions. You can then check with an outside typesetter or bindery if you wish. (Printing and binding, however, are usually handled together, even when typesetting is provided by someone other than the printer.)

Ask the printer about the economies of size. Some sizes of books involve a lot of paper waste, which also means wasted money. Give the printer details of what you will provide (such as 14 double-spaced, typed, and edited chapter manuscripts, each averaging 20 pages—about 280 letter-size manuscript pages in all). Specify how many frontmatter pages there will be (possibly a half-title page, title page, copyright page, preface written by the program chair or conference chair, acknowledgments page, and table of contents) and how many backmatter pages there will be (possibly a glossary and a subject index). Time is often so short, however, that organizations omit the glossary and index. But the frontmatter will take less time to prepare, and it's essential if you really want the book to look like a book. Besides, the Planning Committee may have instructed you to copyright the book, so you'll need a copyright page at the front of the book in any case.

Let the printer know how many photographs there will be and how many line drawings. Be certain that the Program Committee has requested that the speakers submit black and white eight-by-ten-inch glossy photographs and pen and ink (black) line drawings (or computer-prepared black and white graphics). This requirement assumes that your budget won't stretch to cover color in the book—it all must be black and white, even the cover ink (although the cover stock may be colored rather than white).

Finally, describe to the printer how you want to handle proofreading (you want to see proofs after typesetting—galleys and/or pages—as well as negative or press proofs—blueprints, brownlines, or the like—that show the positions of tables, photographs, and other elements). Explain that you have a very tight schedule that absolutely must be met. This isn't a situation in which you can simply postpone the meeting a few days if the books aren't done in time. The completed books *must* be delivered to the conference site on or before the day preceding the opening (ask the Facilities Committee about a preferred delivery date). The printer must guarantee completion and delivery in writing.

What if the quotes you receive are all too high and there is no apparent way to cut corners without sacrificing quality? There is another alternative. Would your company be willing to have the staff that prepares your company house organ also prepare the edited manuscript pages by computer? You could then supply either diskettes or a camera-ready printout to the printer. Suppose that your company, as a member of the organization sponsoring the meeting, agrees to make this contribution (you will credit the company in the acknowledgments of the book), and the Planning Committee is in full agreement. This eliminates the typesetting cost, so you now have to consider only printing, binding, and transportation to the conference site.

All of the quotes you receive may be similar, but one is usually lower than the others. There are other considerations, though. Does the printer have book-production experience? Have you seen samples of its work? Does it have a reputation for meeting deadlines? After you've considered all factors, select the firm that you believe can do the best job (it may not have the lowest cost) and submit your recommendation to the finance chair and the Planning Committee. Once this preliminary work is finished and you have authorization to proceed, be certain that the printer you select has clarified in writing everything that will be supplied along with the associated costs and your timetable. After you accept the written proposal (in writing), you can start work on the papers from speakers as they arrive.

The sponsoring organization may have its own style book or may use another particular style book for all of its written and printed material. If you are expected to select a style for the book, however, choose a style book that is appropriate for your field (the *Council of Biology Editors Style Manual*, for example, is appropriate for certain scientific works). One of the most popular style books used in publishing is the *Chicago Manual of Style*.

Edit all papers to be consistent with the style you choose. If you are uncertain how to edit a manuscript, find an example to follow. The *Chicago Manual of Style* has a section titled "How to Mark a Manuscript," with a sample page of edited manuscript. In the same book you'll also find details on book design (type specifications, page layout, and so on).

If your company is setting the pages, either give the operators your specifications to follow or ask them to submit sample pages that show a suggested type style, spacing (around headings and other elements), chapter titles and subheads, footnotes, and other parts of each chapter. If the appearance doesn't suit you, ask for changes and new sample pages. Find out how the computer operators would like to have the pages marked in regard to the design. They may want you to mark the various elements on each page so that they know what type size and layout to use for each one. You might use letters that you could circle beside each element on a manuscript page: CT = chapter title; A = first-level subhead; B = second-level subhead; C = third-level subhead; UT = unnumbered table; L = numbered list; ML = multicolumn list; FN = footnote; SN = source note; and so on. At the end, every element on each page should be keyed; the computer operator shouldn't have to guess what something is or what type should be used for it or how it should be set up on the page.

Each quote in a speaker's paper should have a source (a footnote at the bottom of the page or note in a list of reference notes at the end of the chapter). An illustration being reprinted from a copyrighted source must have a source note and permission to use it in this book. (Ask the Program Committee to advise speakers—before they prepare their papers—that they must submit letters of permission from the owners of copyrighted material used in a paper. If you're preparing a set of instructions for speakers, be certain to include this.) Write to the Library of Congress in Washington, D.C., and ask for forms with instructions for copyrighting a book; when the first printed copies are available, follow the copyright instructions precisely before you do anything else—if you don't do it correctly, the copyright will be lost, and the work will fall into the public domain.

Continue to work closely with the Program Committee in regard to the order of topics in the book (probably to match the order on the program) and late papers. In the meantime, after you've approved the page design and type specifications and have a few papers edited, the computer operators can begin keyboarding. Thereafter, as you finish editing each paper, submit it to the operators. If they're handling the graphics, submit illustrations along with each paper; otherwise, if the printer is handling the graphics, illustrations should be carefully keyed for position in the various chapters before submitting them to the printer for processing. (So that you don't crease a photograph, use a grease pencil to make crop marks in the white borders or a felt-tip pen to write on the back of the photograph. For lengthy comments or instructions, attach a separate piece of paper to a photograph.)

Keep a style sheet as you edit, noting how you are marking things such as numbers (*ten* or *10*), prefixes (*nontraditional* or *non-traditional*), and suffixes (*sandlike* or *sand-like*); how you are treating footnotes (paragraph indent or flush left, raised numbers or numbers on line) and other elements; how special terms are capitalized (*Republican party* or *Republican Party*); and anything else that might occur in the manuscript, such as setting quotes of eight lines or more as indented extracts. Don't trust your memory to capitalize, spell, hyphenate, and style all words, titles, and so on the same in every chapter. A style sheet is essential for any editor (or writer).

Although the computer operator may use a spell-checker to correct errors, you should still proofread every page. Some copy may have been omitted or paragraphs typed out of order. Also, a spell-checker would not catch all errors. If someone types *the* for *then*, the computer will assume *the* is correct. Use a proofreading guide to mark the proofs you are reading. Charts with symbols to use in marking proofs can be found in most style books. The *Chicago Manual of Style*, for example, has a list of the marks to use along with a sample page of marked proof. Whereas one marks directly on or between the lines of type on a manuscript page, proofreader marks are placed in the margins on a page proof or galley.

While all of this is going on, monitor the schedule closely. Is everyone meeting the deadlines for each part of the job? Usually, there is little time to spare, and if any papers are late, you'll probably be behind schedule.

Be certain that you see proofs of everything, including negative or press proofs, before the pages are printed, or you may find that a photograph belonging on page five in the first chapter somehow got printed on page sixty-seven in the fourth chapter. Whether your company or the printer is designing the cover, insist on seeing a layout and then a proof for it as well. Finally, monitor the concluding stages of production through binding and check with the printer to ensure that the bound copies are being shipped to the conference site on schedule.

As soon as the frontmatter is available, send in the copyright-registration form. Deliver advance copies to the Program Committee and the Planning Committee, and advise the Registration and Facilities committees that copies are being delivered to the conference site (the Facilities Committee in conjunction with the hotel should arrange for storage until the conference opens, and the Registration Committee will likely be in charge of proceedings handouts or sales to registrants).

After the meeting, or upon completion of the printing job, review final bills and forward them to the designated person for payment. File your style sheet, the design specifications, and other material related to the production in a meeting folder for use by future meeting arrangers and submit a concluding report to the Planning Committee.

MEETING CONDUCT: THE NEW ROBERT'S RULES OF ORDER

Introduction to the Rules

IN THE PREFACE to the 1893 edition of *Robert's Rules of Order*, General H. M. Robert began by stating that "a work on parliamentary law has long been needed, based, in its general principles, upon the rules and practice of Congress, but adapted, in its details, to the use of ordinary societies." If he were writing this introduction he would probably begin by stating that "a work on parliamentary law is needed as much today as it was in 1893." Perhaps it is needed even more, since there are more people and more organized bodies holding meetings than ever before.

The importance of the 1893 edition and the validity of its content here have never been contested, and *The New Robert's Rules of Order* is a testimony to its worth rather than an indictment of its diminished value. Although some changes have occurred in the rules of parliamentary procedure, the original rules, by and large, still apply. However, a lot of other things have changed in the world since 1893. Perhaps most obvious are changes in the written and spoken language that we use. Some people, especially school-age readers and young adults in the working world, are distracted and confused by the writing style that was appropriate nearly a hundred years ago. To some, then, the meaning of the text is lost in the prose. This points to a principal aim of *The New Robert's Rules of Order:* to present all of General Robert's rules and commentary in contemporary English.

The complete and official text of the 1893 edition included notes appended to the various sections, highlighting rule changes that had occurred since General Robert's first book of rules had been published in 1876.

Whereas such revisions appear as separate "Notes" in the 1893 version, they're blended into the text in *The New Robert's Rules of Order* so the updated information is conveyed in a less obtrusive, easier to comprehend style. The changes, then, are no longer presented as notes to the main text but are treated as the updated text itself.

One thing has not been changed in *The New Robert's Rules of Order:* the organization of the contents. Although persuasive arguments could be developed for changing the organization of material, one important factor prevailed—the objective of this new version is to simplify and clarify the original text so that readers can follow and comprehend it more easily. Therefore, we didn't want to do anything that might confuse anyone, and changing the order of topics to which readers have become accustomed over the years could well invite confusion. If you are at a meeting and a question arises, you may want to discuss with others a certain point in the book of rules. If the appropriate section is numbered 15 in your book and 21 in someone else's edition, it will cause unnecessary delay. So in the interest of consistency, this version retains the same order of topics, the same chapter and article titles, and the same section numbers as the 1893 edition. Only the text within each section has been rewritten in a modern, more readable style.

Like the 1893 edition, this edition also divides the text information on parliamentary procedure into three parts: I. Rules of Order; II. Organization and Conduct of Business; and III. Miscellaneous. Part I gives the traditional rules of order and discusses rules about the introduction of business at a meeting, the classification of motions, the precedence of motions, the role of committees, procedures for debate, voting methods, the role of officers and the minutes, and miscellaneous related items such as quorum requirements. Each rule in Part I is complete in itself or refers to every other section in the book that qualifies it. Part II discusses topics in relation to matters of organization and the conduct of business—for example, organization and meetings, officers and committees, the introduction of business, motions, and miscellaneous items such as forms (wording) of putting questions to a vote. This part of the book offers a simple explanation of the common methods of conducting business in ordinary meetings. Motions here are classified according to use and compared with others. This part is useful for people who can't devote a lot of time to the intricacies of parliamentary law but want to feel confident that they can function intelligently at a meeting. Part III is a final miscellaneous section discussing other matters such as punishment of members and the legal rights of assemblies. Following the three main parts, just before the main index at the end of the book, is a quick-reference table of motions for use during meetings.

For a more complete list of topics, refer to the table of contents in the front of the book and, especially, to the general index at the end of the book. For information about meeting matters other than parliamentary procedure, review the chapters at the beginning of the book concerning meeting arrangements.

Parliamentary Law

Originally, *parliamentary law* referred to the customs and rules of conducting business in the English Parliament. Now, in the United States, it also refers to the customs and rules of conducting business in U.S. legislative assemblies. As long as these customs and rules don't conflict with other rules or precedents that already exist, they're considered *the* authority for the conduct of business in assembled groups.

U.S. organizations, however, have different needs from those of the English Parliament, and the rules have been changed from time to time to fit those needs. Individual organizations in the United States have also modified the rules to fit their own particular needs. On the national level, the House of Representatives, for instance, doesn't use the same rules that the Senate uses. The *exact* method of conducting business in any organization, therefore, depends on that organization's specific needs, legal requirements, and established rules and precedents.

Parliamentary law in the United States has thus superseded English parliamentary law in ordinary deliberative assemblies—that is, in the many organized groups (other than formal U.S. legislative bodies) that assemble to conduct business. These bodies—assemblies of all types and sizes from those of small local clubs to large national organizations—have needed some system of conducting business and a set of rules to govern their proceedings. The unique system of parliamentary law developed in the United States has thus become the "common law" of these ordinary deliberative assemblies. However, even though U.S. parliamentary law differs from English parliamentary law, and even though the two houses of Congress follow different rules in some respects, the *final* authority for all great parliamentary questions (such as what motions can be made and what is the proper order of precedence or which ones can be debated and what is their effect) is the practice of the U.S. House of Representatives—not the Senate, the English Parliament, or any other body.

The rules of the House, then, are considered a greater authority than those of the Senate in determining parliamentary law in the United States. For instance, the Senate rules don't allow one to make a motion calling for the Previous Question [asking that debate stop and a matter be brought to a vote] (Section 20), and they make a motion to Postpone [a matter] Indefinitely (Section 24) take precedence over every other subsidiary motion (see Section 7) except to Lay [a matter] on the Table (Section 19). But the House recognizes the Previous Question as a legitimate motion and assigns the motion to Postpone Indefinitely to the very lowest rank. In other matters of detail, though, ordinary deliberative assemblies wouldn't necessarily follow the House rules. The chair in the House, for example, can order that the galleries be cleared or that a bill must be read three times before its passage. Such matters are inappropriate for other organizations. Yet, in conducting business, when an organization can't decide a case clearly or easily, it should imitate the rules of the legislative bodies.

Plan of the Work

The rules of order in this book are suitable for ordinary deliberative assemblies (nonlegislative bodies). They should be sufficient for most organizations until they need to adopt other rules to meet some special requirement. The rules are based on the practice of Congress except when the practice is not appropriate for ordinary assemblies (even then the rules in Congress are given for comparison). In important matters, the rules given here are used by the House of Representatives.

One of the exceptions to House rules recommended for ordinary assemblies concerns the vote required to pass a measure. The House uses a bare majority to take final action on a question without allowing any discussion. But ordinary groups need to consider the rights of minorities; they should require a two-thirds vote to sustain an objection to introducing a question or to adopt a motion calling for the Previous Question (Section 20) or to adopt an order closing or limiting debate (see Section 39). In this book a majority is needed to order a vote by "yeas and nays" (see Section 38), and this rule is best for most assemblies. Congress, on the other hand, needs only a one-fifth vote, and in some groups a single member can require that a vote be taken by "yeas and nays." An organization, therefore, should use the rules given here whenever they're appropriate and as long as they're consistent with the group's own rules of order and bylaws (see Section 49 for the form of a rule that an organization can adopt for this purpose). An organization's own rules should cover all of those cases when it's necessary to depart from the rules in this book and, especially, should provide for a quorum (see Section 43) and an order of business (see Section 44).

The text is divided into three distinct parts, followed

by a quick-reference section including a table of rules for easy reference in the midst of the business of a meeting.

Part I

The first part has a set of rules arranged systematically (as shown in the table of contents) in forty-five sections. Each section is complete in itself so that you can examine selected subjects without being misled. However, each section also has cross-references to other sections that are related or are important to the subject under consideration.

The motions are arranged by order of rank under their traditional classes. (Note, however, that motions are listed *alphabetically* in the index at the back of the book.) The following information is given in regard to each motion:

- A list of other motions over which a particular motion takes precedence (i.e., motions that may be pending while it is nevertheless proper [in order] to make and consider a particular motion)

- Other motions to which a particular motion yields (i.e., motions that may be made and considered while a particular motion is pending)

- Whether the motion is debatable (all motions are debatable unless stated otherwise)

- Whether a motion can be amended

- Which motions cannot have a subsidiary motion applied to them (see Section 11, Adjourn, for an example: the motion to Adjourn can't be laid on the table, postponed, committed, or amended)

- The effect of a motion, if adopted, when it might be misunderstood

- The form of stating a question (motion) when it's unusual and any other information necessary to understand the question

Part II

The second part is a parliamentary primer. It gives simple illustrations of the methods of organizing and conducting different kinds of meetings and the sample wording to follow when making and putting motions to a vote. It also outlines the duties of officers, the forms of minutes, and the forms of treasurer and committee reports. Finally, it classifies the motions in eight categories according to their objective, examines each class and compares the motions in it, and explains when each motion should be used.

Part III

The third part discusses miscellaneous matters that are important to assemblies, including the commonly misunderstood subjects of the legal rights of deliberative assemblies or ecclesiastical tribunals.

Quick-Reference Guide to Motions

After the third part and just before the main index at the back of the book is a table of rules about motions for quick reference during a meeting. This is followed by a list showing the precedence of motions and a list of forms (wording) for putting certain questions, or motions, to a vote.

Definitions and Common Errors

To avoid misunderstanding when you read the following text, note the special meanings of the following terms:

Accepting a Report. Adopting (not receiving) a report (see Section 30 for common errors in acting on reports).

Assembly. An organized body meeting to conduct business. When making a motion, substitute the term that applies to your group: *society, board, convention,* and so on.

Congress. Generally, in reference to rules, the U.S. House of Representatives (not the Senate).

Meeting and Session. The word *meeting* refers to an assembly of members gathered for any length of time without adjournment. A *session* includes all of the adjourned meetings (see Section 42).

Previous Question. A motion calling for an end to debate and requiring that a vote be taken on the pending question (see Section 20).

Shall the Question Be Discussed. A common form of stating the question about considering a subject; a negative vote dismisses the matter for that session (see Section 15).

Substitute. This motion is one form of an amendment. The five forms are given in note 3 to the table of rules in the Quick-Reference Guide (see also Section 23).

Part I. Rules of Order

SINCE THIS PART thoroughly covers the rules of order, some of you will be primarily interested in this material, especially if you already have a basic knowledge of parliamentary law. But if the rules seem difficult to understand at first reading, skip over to Part II, which is a parliamentary primer, and read it first; then return to Part I.

Article I. Introduction of Business

Section 1. Introducing Business

There are two ways that you can bring business before an assembled group: make a motion or present a communication. You can also make a motion to receive communications or committee reports. But groups that are gathered for a meeting (often referred to as an *assembly* in this book) may dispense with the formality of such a motion; however, if a member of the assembly objects to doing that, the group will have to act by way of a regular motion.

Section 2. Obtaining the Floor

Before you can make a motion or address the assembly on any matter, you have to "obtain the floor." This means that you have to stand up (in a formal setting) and address the presiding officer (referred to as the "chair" in this book) by his or her title, for example:

Madam President
Mr. Chairman

The chair will then recognize you by announcing your name or (if not known) by nodding in your direction:

The chair recognizes Ms. Davis.

But if the chair rises to speak before you obtain the floor, you must take your seat for the time being (see Section 36).

If you're conducting the meeting, it's up to you to recognize the member trying to get your attention. But what if two or more persons stand up at the same time? Who is entitled to the floor—that is, to speak to the assembly? (If there are any doubts about who should have the floor, you can always allow the assembly to decide by vote, with the person receiving the largest vote obtaining the floor.) Robert's rules of order recommend that you be guided by these principles in making a decision:

- Recognize the person who previously made a motion being discussed or the one who presented a committee report currently under discussion (unless he or she already has had the floor during the discussion), even though another individual may have stood up and addressed the chair first.

- No one who has had the floor previously may have it again while the same question is before the assembly if someone else who hasn't yet spoken asks to be recognized. (See Section 26 for details on what to do if you want to change the question before an assembly.)

- Make an effort to allow both sides of a question to be presented; if someone has spoken on one side of a measure, try to recognize next someone who will address the other side of the issue.

- Don't recognize someone who stood up and remained standing while another person was speaking if still another individual rises after the speaker finishes and yields the floor.

If others object to your decision in recognizing someone, any two members can appeal your decision. But the House of Representatives doesn't allow such an appeal, and in other large assemblies, too, such an appeal is not desirable, since the chair needs to have more power to handle a large group and maintain order.

Once the floor is assigned to someone, no one—neither you (the chair) nor another member of the assembly—should interrupt that person by calling for the question (a vote on a motion), by making a motion to Adjourn (Section 11), or by doing anything else. (But see the exceptions listed below.) A chair, then, should try to protect the rights of a speaker who has the floor.

> *Ms. Jackson:* Therefore, we need to consider other alternatives.

> *Mr. Barnes:* Mr. Chairman, I move that we adjourn this meeting.

> *Chair:* Sir, you are out of order. Ms. Jackson has the floor.

There are five exceptions to the rule about not interrupting a member who has been given the floor; it may be necessary to interrupt someone for these reasons:

1. To enter in the minutes a motion to Reconsider (Section 27)

2. To allow a question of order (see Section 14)

3. To recognize an Objection to the Consideration of a Question (Section 15)

4. To call for Orders of the Day (Section 13)

5. To admit a Question of Privilege that requires immediate action (see Section 12)

A person who interrupts for a legitimate reason should state his or her purpose for doing so:

> **Mr. Chairman, I rise to a point of order [*want to point out a breach of parliamentary rules*].**

Assume that a member obtains the floor and makes a motion that is in order (allowed) and is debatable. If that motion isn't seconded immediately, you, as chair, should ask:

> **Does anyone want to second the motion to ____?**

A member can second it, without rising, by simply stating:

> **I second the motion to ____.**

Until members have had time to second a motion, you shouldn't allow any other motion to be made. Even then, after the first motion is seconded, no one should make a new motion until the person who made the first one decides to yield the floor; in fact, you might ask:

> **Will Mr. Billingsley yield the floor now?**

Motions to Adjourn (Section 11) and to Lay [a matter] on the Table (Section 19) are often made incorrectly (a) by persons who don't have the floor, (b) after someone has just made another motion, and (c) while the person making the other motion is still entitled to the floor. A chair shouldn't recognize such new motions. (But see Article III on motions and their order of precedence.)

A person who submits a committee report or offers a resolution doesn't lose the floor by asking the secretary to read it. The secretary doesn't thereby gain the floor—and the chair can't accept a motion made by the secretary—unless the person who submits the report or resolution yields the floor. Usually, after the secretary finishes reading, the person submitting the material resumes the floor and makes a motion that it be adopted. The chair would recognize the person as having the floor and would state the question (repeat the motion). However, a member who wants to make a motion that is "in order" (proper) when someone else has the floor could interrupt that person at any time. (See the table of rules and list of precedence of motions in the Quick-Reference Guide.)

Section 3. What Precedes Debate on a Question

Before any subject is open to debate (see Section 34), three things are necessary:

1. A motion must be made by a member who has the floor (see Section 46 for examples of various forms of making motions):

   I move that we adopt the Maxwell proposal.

2. The motion must be seconded:

   I second the motion.

   Exceptions: A call for Orders of the Day (Section 13), a question of order but not an Appeal (Section 14), and an Objection to the Consideration of a Question (Section 15) do not have to be seconded. (In Congress, motions don't have to be seconded; even in ordinary assemblies, routine motions are not always made, and some are never seconded; the presiding officer merely announces that, if no one objects, the matter will be considered the action of the assembly.)

3. The motion must be stated by the presiding officer (see Section 65 for forms of stating questions):

   The motion to adopt the Maxwell proposal has been seconded. It's now open to debate.

Before the chair states the question, though, the person making a motion can modify or withdraw it. *After* the chair states it, the person must get the consent of the assembly to modify or withdraw it (see Sections 5 and 17). When a person withdraws or modifies a motion, the member who seconded it can withdraw his or her second. The series of remarks might resemble this:

Ms. Adams: I move that we adopt the Maxwell proposal.

Mr. Brubaker: I second the motion.

Ms. Adams: Before the chair reads the motion, I'd like to modify it to read: "I move we adopt the Maxwell proposal as amended on January 9, 19XX."

Mr. Brubaker: I then withdraw my second.

Chair: Does anyone want to second Ms. Adam's modified statement?

Mr. Donatelli: I second the modified motion.

Chair: The motion to adopt the Maxwell proposal as amended on January 9, 19XX, is seconded. It's now open to debate.

Section 4. What Motions Must Be in Writing and How They Should Be Divided

All principal motions (see Section 6), amendments, and instructions to committees should be in writing—if required by the presiding officer. Sometimes a question is complicated and could be simplified by dividing it into several less complex questions. But unless a special rule allows a member to ask for this to be done, he or she can't insist on it. Instead, anyone who wants this done should make a motion to that effect and indicate in the motion how the particular matter can be divided. But someone else can then make another motion, as an amendment, to divide it differently.

Division of a Question. The division of a question is really an amendment and subject to the same rules (see Section 23). Therefore, instead of moving to divide a question, you could make a motion for some other form of amendment.

For a question to be divided, each separate question that results must be something the assembly can act on even if the other resulting questions aren't adopted. A motion to Commit (Section 22) with instructions, therefore, can't be divided because if the motion to Commit should fail, the motion to instruct the committee wouldn't make sense (there wouldn't be any committee to instruct).

According to Rule 46 of the House, a question must be divided upon the demand of one member if it "comprehends propositions in substance so distinct that one being taken away a substantive proposition shall remain for the decision of the House." This doesn't mean that a question can be divided just to enable a vote on separate items or names. Rule 121, however, states that one-fifth of the members can demand a vote on separate or collective items, as specified in the call, in the case of a bill making appropriations for internal improvements. But this right to divide a question into items extends only to the case specified. Common parliamentary law doesn't allow for division unless the assembly orders it, and in ordinary assemblies, this rule is more appropriate than that of the House.

A motion to strike out certain words and insert others can't be divided because, usually, the two steps belong together; that is, both must occur to make sense.

Section 5. Modifications of a Motion by Mover

After a chair has stated a question (motion), it's open to debate by members of the assembly. The person making the motion can no longer withdraw or modify it, if anyone objects, without getting the approval of the assembly to withdraw it (see Section 17) or by making a motion for an amendment (see Section 3).

According to Rule 40 of the House: "After a motion is stated by the Speaker, or read by the Clerk, it shall be deemed to be in the possession of the House, but may be withdrawn at any time before a decision or amendment." The practice in the House has been *not* to allow a motion to be withdrawn after the Previous Question (Section 20) has been seconded. The rules of order in this book conform to the old parliamentary principle, which is more suitable for ordinary assemblies. Some groups, though, may prefer to follow the practice of the House.

Article II. General Classification of Motions

Section 6. Principal, or Main, Motions

A *principal*, or *main, motion*, also known as a principal, or main, question, is a motion on any particular subject brought before an assembly for consideration. You can't make a principal motion when another motion, or question, is before the assembly. Since a principal motion does *not* have precedence over any other motion, it yields to all secondary motions, incidental motions, and privileged motions (see Sections 7, 8, and 9). Also, any motion is out of order if it conflicts with the organization's constitution, bylaws, standing orders, or resolutions, as well as any resolution adopted during the sessions (see Section 42). Such a motion might be adopted in error, but it would be null and void. To introduce such a motion, the assembly would have to rescind any conflicting rule or resolution or amend the constitution or bylaws. (Note that the motion to Reconsider [Section 27] isn't a principal motion; it's a motion that brings a matter before the assembly again.)

Section 7. Subsidiary, or Secondary, Motions

A *subsidiary*, or *secondary, motion* is a motion applied to another motion as a means of disposing of the other motion (in other words, the two motions are made together at the same time).

> *Example:* A motion to have an Appeal (Section 14) Lay on the Table (Section 19) is a secondary motion because it enables the assembly to dispose of the Appeal. The Appeal, meanwhile, is an incidental question that arises because some members object to a decision of the chair.

A subsidiary motion has precedence over a principal motion and has to be decided before the assembly can act on the principal motion. But a subsidiary motion yields to privileged and incidental questions (see Sections 8 and 9). The six subsidiary motions are listed here in order of precedence:

1. Lay on the Table (Section 19)

2. Previous Question (Section 20)

3. Postpone to a Certain Day (Section 21)

4. Commit or Refer (Section 22)

5. Amend (Section 23)

6. Postpone Indefinitely (Section 24)

You can make any of these subsidiary motions except the one to Amend when another lower-order motion is pending. But you can't make a subsidiary motion if one of a higher order is pending. Subsidiary motions can't be "applied" to one another except in the following cases:

- The Previous Question can be applied to the motion to Postpone without affecting the principal motion and can, if specified, be applied to a pending amendment (see Section 20).

- The motions to Postpone to a Certain Day, to Commit, and to Amend can be amended.

- A motion to Amend a certain part of the minutes can be laid on the table (see Section 19) without carrying all of the minutes with it.

Section 8. Incidental Motions

Incidental motions arise out of other motions and, therefore, take precedence over and must be decided before these other motions. But they yield to privileged questions (see Section 9) and can't be amended. All incidental motions except an Appeal are undebatable; an Appeal may or may not be debated (see Section 14). The five incidental motions are listed here in order of precedence:

1. Appeal, or Questions of Order (Section 14)

2. Objection to Consideration of a Question (Section 15)

3. Reading Papers (Section 16)

4. Withdrawal of a Motion (Section 17)

5. Suspend the Rules (Section 18)

Section 9. Privileged Motions

Privileged motions are not related to a pending question but, because of their importance, take precedence over all other motions. They can't be debated (see Section 35) unless they pertain to the rights of the assembly or its members; therefore, they can't be used to interrupt business. The four privileged motions are listed here in order of precedence:

1. Fix the Time to Which to Adjourn (Section 10)

2. Adjourn (Section 11)

3. Questions of Privilege (Section 12)

4. Call for Orders of the Day (Section 13)

Article III. Motions and Their Order of Precedence

The ordinary motions are arranged in order of precedence in the Precedence of Motions list in the Quick-Reference Guide to Motions. The privileged motions (see Sections 10–13) and the subsidiary motions (see Sections 19–24) are discussed here in order of precedence.

Privileged Motions

Section 10. To Fix the Time to Which to Adjourn

The motion to Fix the Time to Which to Adjourn takes precedence over all other motions. In fact, this motion is in order even after the assembly has voted to adjourn provided the chair hasn't yet announced the result of the vote on adjournment. If you make a motion to Fix the Time to Which to Adjourn when another question is before the assembly, it's not debatable (see Section 35). It can be amended, though, by altering the time. If you make this motion when no other question is before the assembly, it's treated the same as any other principal motion and in that case *is* debatable.

In ordinary groups it's best to follow common parliamentary law and introduce this motion as a principal motion. Then it can be debated or suppressed (see Sections 58 and 59) like other questions. (In Congress, however, this motion can't be debated under any circumstances, and there it has entirely superseded the unprivileged and inferior motion to Adjourn to a particular time.)

The correct form for stating the motion to Fix the Time to Which to Adjourn is as follows:

That when this assembly adjourns, it adjourns to meet at ___ time.

Section 11. To Adjourn

The motion to Adjourn, when it's not qualified, takes precedence over all others except the motion to Fix the Time to Which to Adjourn (Section 10). The motion to Adjourn can't be debated or amended, and it can't have a subsidiary motion (see Section 7) applied to it. Also a vote on adjournment can't be reconsidered. When a motion to Adjourn is qualified in some way, it loses its status as a privileged motion and becomes simply another principal motion.

You can repeat the motion to Adjourn if other business has intervened or if debate has progressed (see Section 26). But you can't make a motion to Adjourn if someone else has the floor. Also, you can't make this motion after another question has been stated and is being put to a vote, but you can make the motion after the vote has been taken and before it has been announced. If that happens, the chair should announce the vote after business has resumed.

Sometimes, with elections and other time-consuming matters, it's best for a group to take a short recess (or transact other business) until the tellers have counted the ballots and are ready to report. (A *recess* is an adjournment of a group for a limited time during a session.) For example, you might move:

> **That when we adjourn, we adjourn to meet at the call of the chair.**

The chair would then call the meeting to order as soon as the ballots are counted. Or you could move to take a recess of fifteen (or other) minutes. This would be in order unless there is a pending motion to Adjourn or a question has been "put" and the assembly is voting on it.

An assembly may vote down a motion to Adjourn if the participants want to hear another speech or take another vote. But since that's true, it's necessary to be able to renew the motion afterward. The chair, however, should take steps to ensure that this privilege isn't abused. If you were conducting a meeting, for example, and the group had just voted down a motion to Adjourn, you should refuse to consider another motion to Adjourn if nothing had yet occurred. The group in this case presumably would still not want to adjourn until other business was transacted. Also, as chair, you shouldn't consider any appeal or questions of order after someone moved to Adjourn unless the assembly voted down the motion.

Some business is referred to committees. When a committee is through with any business referred to it and is ready to report, someone should make a motion to Rise. This motion in a committee has the same privileges as a motion to Adjourn in an assembly.

An adjournment affects unfinished business as follows:

- When some unfinished business occurs at the end of a meeting but not at the close of a session, it should be the first order of business, after the reading of the minutes, at the next meeting in that session. It then would be treated as though there had been no adjournment. (An *adjourned meeting* is legally the continuation of a meeting that had previously adjourned to meet later.) The assembly, however, may adopt rules that modify this general rule.

- When some unfinished business occurs at the end of a session and the assembly has more than one regular session each year, the unfinished business is taken up at the next session, before the introduction of "new business," and it's still treated as though there had been no adjournment (see Section 44 for its place in the order of business). But in a body elected for a specific term (one year, for example), unfinished business is simply dropped at the end of the term.

- When an adjournment closes a session in an assembly that meets only once a year, or when the assembly is an elective body, and the session ends the term of some of the members, the unfinished business also ends at the close of the session. But it can be introduced at the next session as if it had never been before the assembly.

According to Rule 136 of the House, after six days from the beginning of a second or subsequent session of any Congress, all bills, resolutions, and reports that originated in the House and are undecided at the close of the next preceding session must be resumed and acted on as though there had been no adjournment. But unfinished business doesn't go from one Congress to another. Any ordinary society that meets only once a year would likely have a different membership each year (just as each new congressional composition may be different). In that case, it would be unwise for it to carry unfinished business to a future year.

Section 12. Questions of Privilege

Questions of Privilege are motions pertaining to the rights and privileges of the assembly, or any of its members. They take precedence over all other questions except the motions to Fix the Time to Which to Adjourn (Section 10) and to Adjourn (Section 11). But Questions of Privilege aren't the same thing as privileged questions. (Privileged questions include Questions of Privilege; see Section 9.) Examples of Questions of Privilege are disorder in the gallery, one member opening a window and causing a draft that endangers the health of others, or charges against the official character of a member. For instance:

Mr. Wright (speaker): I therefore recommend that . . .

Member (interrupting): Madam President, I move that the window just opened along the left aisle be closed. The cold wind is bothering those of us in its path.

President: Will the member seated by the window please close it? You may continue, Mr. Wright.

If a Question of Privilege requires immediate action, it can interrupt a member's speech. But the chair must decide if a question is really a Question of Privilege. Even if the chair rules that it is, any two members can appeal that decision.

Suppose that an assembly doesn't want to take final action on a Question of Privilege when it's raised. The question, then, might be referred to a committee (see Section 22). Or it might be laid on the table (see Section 19). Or it might have another subsidiary motion (see Section 7) applied to it. In that case, the subsidiary motion would be decided (disposed of) without affecting the question that was interrupted by the Question of Privilege. As soon as the Question of Privilege is disposed of, the assembly may return to considering the original question that was interrupted.

Section 13. Orders of the Day

Orders of the Day refers to the assignment of subjects in a meeting. A call for the Orders of the Day takes precedence over every other motion except the motions to Reconsider (Section 27), to Fix the Time to Which to Adjourn (Section 10), and to Adjourn (Section 11) and except for Questions of Privilege (Section 12). A call for the Orders of the Day can't be debated and can't be amended. Moreover, it doesn't have to be seconded, and it's in order even when another person has the floor:

Ms. Jacobs (speaker): Unless we act . . .

Mr. Hill (interrupting): Mr. Chairman, I move that we proceed to the orders of the day.

Chair: The chair recognizes Mr. Hill.

Mr. Hill: Mr. Chairman, we were supposed to be considering the Newtown zoning plan.

Chair: Thank you, Mr. Hill. Ms. Jacobs will now yield the floor, and we'll move on to the zoning plan.

Rule 54 of the House provides that at the close of the morning hour devoted to committee reports and resolutions, a motion is in order to move on to "the business on the Speaker's [of the House] table and to the orders of the day." It then specifies the order in which the business will be considered and states that "the messages, communications, and bills on his table having been disposed of, the Speaker shall then proceed to call the orders of the day." Although in Congress it is not in order to interrupt a member to call for the Orders of the Day, at the close of the morning hour a member may, even though someone else has the floor, move to proceed to "the business on the Speaker's table and to the orders of the day." To apply the House principle to ordinary groups, it's necessary to allow a motion for the Orders of the Day to interrupt a member who has the floor after the time has arrived for their consideration.

When one or more subjects have been assigned to a particular day or hour, they become the Orders of the Day for that time. They can't be considered before then except by a two-thirds vote (see Section 39). When the specific time arrives, if the orders are called up, they take precedence over all motions except the ones to Fix the Time to Which to Adjourn (Section 10), to Adjourn (Section 11), and to Reconsider (Section 27) as well as Questions of Privilege (Section 12). But instead of considering the subjects at that time, the assembly could appoint another time for their consideration. If a matter isn't taken up at the new time, then, the order is dropped.

Orders of the Day involve two classes: General Orders and Special Orders. The Special Orders always take precedence over the General Orders.

General Orders. These orders can be made by a majority by postponing questions to certain times or by adopting a program or order of business for the day or session. The General Orders, however, must not interfere with any established rules of an assembly.

Special Orders. A Special Order suspends all of the rules of an assembly that interfere with its consideration at the time specified. It therefore requires a two-thirds vote to make any question a Special Order. (If a group had adopted the order of business as described in Section 44, when the specified time arrived, anyone could call for Special Orders even though a committee might be reporting at the time. But the Orders for the Day in general could not be called for until all of the committee's reports had been acted on.)

A call for Special Orders is in order whenever a motion to Suspend the Rules (Section 18) is in order. Once a Special Order is made for a particular time, it's not in order to make another Special Order that would precede or interfere with the first one. Yet a Special Order may interfere with General Orders.

When the Orders of the Day are taken up, the Special Orders must be considered first and then the General Orders. Within each class—Special or General Orders—the individual questions must be taken up in their exact order. If two or more questions are assigned to the same day or hour, the one that was assigned first takes precedence over the others. (A motion to take up a particular part of the Orders of the Day, or a certain question, is not a privileged motion.) Any subject, when taken up, can be assigned to another time instead of being considered then. A majority can postpone even a Special Order.

The correct form of this question as put by the chair when the proper time arrives—or on the call of a member—would be similar to the examples shown here:

Shall the Orders of the Day be taken up?

Will the assembly now proceed to the Orders of the Day?

An *affirmative* vote on a call for the Orders of the Day effectively removes any question being considered by the assembly the same as if it had been interrupted by an adjournment (see Section 11). A *negative* vote on the call effectively stops the orders from interfering with a consideration of the question before the assembly.

When one subject is being considered and the time assigned to another subject arrives, the chair should announce that it's time to move on to the next assigned subject, putting the other question before the assembly to an immediate vote. But if a member objects to moving on, the chair should ask:

Will the assembly now proceed to consider [*subject*] that was assigned to this hour?

Since it takes a formal vote (except by unanimous consent) to proceed to the Orders of the Day, it also takes a formal vote afterward to move on to the next assigned topic if anyone objects to closing discussion on the previous topic.

Incidental Motions

Section 14. To Appeal (Questions of Order)

A *Question of Order* is a question or objection by someone concerning some point of order within a motion. It takes precedence over the motion that prompted it, and it has to be decided by the presiding officer without a debate. But a motion can't be ruled out of order after it already has been entertained and debated without objection. An Appeal can be made only at the time of the decision of the chair. At that time, if a member objects to the decision, he or she would state:

I appeal from the decision of the chair.

If the Appeal is seconded, the chair should immediately state the question:

Shall the decision of the chair stand as the judgment of the assembly [*or* "board, society," *and so on*]?

If there's a tie vote, the decision of the chair stands. (See Section 65 for details on the method of stating the question on an Appeal.)

This Appeal yields to privileged questions (see Section 9). It can't be amended. Also, it can't be debated when it relates simply to indecorum (see Section 36), to transgressions of the rules of speaking, or to the priority of business or if it's made while the Previous Question (Section 20) is pending. When a matter is debatable, a member may speak only once. The presiding officer, however, may (without leaving the chair) state the reasons for his or her decision.

If the Appeal is debatable, the motion to Lay [a matter] on the Table (Section 19) and the Previous Question (Section 20) can be applied to the Appeal and, when adopted, will affect nothing but the Appeal (not the matter being appealed). The vote on an Appeal may also be reconsidered (see Section 27). But an Appeal is not in order when another Appeal is pending. (In Congress the usual course in case of an Appeal is to lay it on the table since this effectively kills it and sustains the decision of the chair.)

The presiding officer must enforce the rules and orders of the assembly without debate or delay. A member may, in fact, insist on it:

Madam Chairman, I rise to a point of order.

The person who was speaking when the member interrupted would then sit down, and the chair would ask the member to state his or her point of order. The member might, for instance, state that the speaker was suggesting action that would violate the group's bylaws. The chair would have to make a decision and might overrule the objection and ask the speaker to continue. Or the chair might find the objection to be in order and would then instruct the speaker to conform to the rules. But if the decision is that the speaker's remarks are improper and if someone objects to having the speaker continue, the assembly must vote on the matter.

Perhaps the speaker is not violating any rule but is using improper language. A member might respond:

I call the speaker to order.

The chair would then decide if the speaker's language is in or out of order. In deciding such Questions of Order, a chair might ask the advice of members. In such cases, to avoid the appearance of debate, members should remain seated when giving advice. Another alternative is for the chair to submit the question to the assembly for a vote.

Section 15. Objection to Consideration of a Question

In a meeting, you can object to having the assembly consider any principal, or main, motion (see Section 6) but only when the motion is first introduced, before it has been debated. Such an objection is similar to a Question of Order (see Section 14) in that you can make it while someone else has the floor and it doesn't require a second. Just as the chair can call a member to order, he or she can make a decision about whether the objection is in order. An Objection to Consideration of a Question can't be debated (see Section 35) or amended (see Section 23). It also can't have any subsidiary motion (see Section 7) applied to it.

When someone makes a motion and another member objects to considering it, the chair must immediately put the question to a vote, first stating it in a form such as one of the following:

Will the assembly consider it?

Shall the question be considered [*or* "discussed"]?

If two-thirds of the members vote no (see Section 39), the subject is dropped for that session (see Section 42). If two-thirds vote yes, the discussion continues as though the question had never come up.

The purpose of a motion objecting to the consideration of a question is not to cut off debate; other motions are available for that (see Section 37). The objective is to give the assembly a chance to avoid questions that the members might view as irrelevant, unprofitable, or contentious.

According to Rule 41 of the House, the introduction of questions that the members might want to avoid could be prevented temporarily by a majority vote: "Where any motion or proposition is made, the question 'Will the House now consider it?' shall not be put unless it is demanded by some member or is deemed necessary by the Speaker." (See Section 39.) The English use the Previous Question (Section 20) for a similar purpose.

The question of consideration is seldom raised in Congress. But in other organizations with short sessions and little time for a lot of questions, it's essential that two-thirds of the members be able to throw out subjects they don't want to consider. Ordinary societies often use the form "Shall the question be discussed?"

Section 16. Reading Papers

Members may ask to have papers that are brought before the assembly read once before voting on them. (See Section 8 for the order of precedence of Reading Papers.) When a member asks to have a paper read, clearly for information and not as a delaying tactic, the chair should call for it to be read if no one objects. Except for this, members don't have the right to have just any material read without permission from the assembly. The motion or request to grant such permission can't be debated or amended.

Section 17. Withdrawal of a Motion

When a question is before an assembly and the person who made the motion wants to withdraw or modify it or substitute another motion, the chair should grant permission if no one objects. (See Section 8 for the order of precedence for the Withdrawal of a Motion.) But if someone objects, the chair will have to put the question to a vote on granting the request, or someone can make a motion to grant it. A motion to withdraw some other motion can't be debated or amended. When a motion is withdrawn, the effect is the same as if it had never been made.

According to Rule 40 of the House, in Congress a motion may be withdrawn by the mover before a decision or amendment is made. But in ordinary societies nothing would be gained by varying from the old common law stated in Section 17. (See also Section 5.)

Section 18. Suspension of the Rules

The motion to Suspend the Rules can't be debated; moreover, it can't be amended, and a subsidiary motion (see Section 7) can't be applied to it. Also, a vote on it may not be reconsidered (see Section 27), nor can a motion to Suspend a Rule for the same purpose be renewed (see Section 26) at the same meeting. However, the motion may be made again after an adjournment even when the next meeting is held on the same day. In Congress, though, the motion can't be renewed the same day. (See Section 8 for the order of precedence of this motion.)

The motion to Suspend the Rules applies only to rules of order or standing rules (see Section 49) since an organization's constitution and bylaws can't be suspended even by unanimous consent, unless they provide for their own suspension. But they should never be suspended except in the case of a bylaw relating to the transaction of business, and then the reason for the suspension should be specified.

The rules of an assembly, therefore, must not be suspended except for a definite purpose, and then a two-thirds vote is required. Also, no rule should be suspended, except by unanimous consent, that gives any right to a minority as small as one-third. It would be pointless, for example, to have a rule allowing one-fifth of the members present to order the "yeas and nays" (see Section 38 and 39) if two-thirds could simply suspend that rule.

The correct form of this motion is as follows:

I move to suspend the rules that interfere with ____.

Subsidiary Motions

Section 19. To Lay on the Table

The motion to *Lay on the Table* a particular subject (set it aside temporarily) takes precedence over all other subsidiary questions (see Section 7). But it yields to any incidental motion (see Section 8) or privileged motion (see Section 9). This motion is not debatable and can't be amended or have any other subsidiary motion applied to

it. Also, an affirmative vote on it can't be reconsidered
(see Section 27); it removes the subject from consideration until the assembly votes to take it from the table.

If a member incorrectly makes a motion to Lay on the
Table some question for a specified time, the chair
shouldn't rule it out of order but should recognize and
state it as a motion to Postpone to a Certain Time (Section 21). The motion to Lay [a subject] on the Table
can't be limited in any way. Some of the correct forms of
this motion are shown in these examples:

> **I move to lay the question of ____ on the table.**

> **I move that the matter of ____ be laid on the
> table.**

> **I move that the question of ____ lie on the table.**

When someone wants to take up the question again, one
of the forms here should be followed:

> **I move to take the question of ____ from the
> table.**

> **I move that we now consider the question of
> ____.**

In organizations with sessions of a day or less, occurring as often as monthly, it should be permissible to take
from the table any question that was laid there at the
previous session (see Section 42). In the case of a resolution, however, it would be better to offer it again as a
new resolution.

The motion to Lay [a subject] on the Table has no
privilege, is undebatable, and can't have any other subsidiary motion applied to it. The object of it is to postpone a subject so that it can be taken up at any time at
the same or in a future meeting. You couldn't accomplish
this by a motion to Postpone Indefinitely (Section 24) or
definitely. The motion also is used frequently to suppress
a question (see Section 59) for a particular session; it can
do this as long as there will never be a majority vote to

take it from the table during that session (see Section 42).

The effect of the motion to Lay [a subject] on the Table is to set aside for that entire session (see Section 42) everything that pertains to the subject. (A Question of Privilege [Section 12] doesn't pertain to the subject it may happen to interrupt; consequently, if it were set aside, the motion to Lay on the Table wouldn't carry with it the question that was interrupted.) For example, if an amendment is ordered to lie on the table, the subject to be amended goes there with it. The following cases, though, are exceptions:

- An Appeal (Section 14) that is laid on the table has the effect of sustaining, at least for the time being, the decision of the chair; it doesn't carry the original subject to the table with it.

- When a motion to Reconsider a Question (Section 27) is laid on the table, the original question is left where it was before moving to Reconsider; only the motion to Reconsider is set aside.

- When an amendment to the minutes is laid on the table, it doesn't carry the entire minutes with it.

Even after a call for the Previous Question (Section 20) brings a matter under discussion to an immediate vote, from the time of ordering the Previous Question until the moment of taking the last vote under it, it still is in order to Lay on the Table the question that was being discussed.

The motion to Lay [a question] on the Table has high privileges. It outranks every debatable question, is undebatable itself, and requires only a majority vote for adoption. An organization needs a motion such as this so that it can instantly put aside certain business and attend to more urgent matters. But in parliamentary law, the reasoning is that every motion that suppresses a question for the session should be open to free debate (see Section 35) unless such debate is limited or closed by at least a two-thirds vote (see Section 39). In assemblies that last only a few hours a bare majority may lay an objectionable question on the table and thereby suppress it without permitting debate; this is an abuse of the motion that often disturbs the harmony of voluntary groups. The motion to Lay on the Table has such high privileges because the assumption is that a question will be set aside only temporarily. Although the motion is valuable when used legitimately, it should require a two-thirds vote if it's going to be used habitually to suppress questions. The following example suggests a partial remedy for the unfair use of the motion.

Example: If you introduce a resolution and then are cut off from speaking by another motion to Lay on the Table the matter you proposed, you should follow this procedure: Immediately claim the floor, which you had and to which you were entitled (see Section 2), and make your speech. Often people who move for a question to be laid on the table are in such a hurry that they fail to address the chair and thereby obtain the floor properly. In such case, you should quickly address the chair, making a point of order— you were the first one to address the chair and the member who interrupted you failed to do so and, not having the floor, isn't entitled to make a motion. Hence it's your right to continue. An alert chair will realize what has happened and should act immediately as shown here:

Mr. Boyle: Therefore, I propose that . . .

Mrs. Solomon (interrupting): I move that we lay this question on the table.

Chair: Mrs. Solomon has not been recognized by the chair. Mr. Boyle, you still have the floor. Please continue.

Motions laid on the table are merely put aside temporarily. Thus if enough members of the majority leave, the minority could all stay until the moment of final adjournment and by then might be in the majority. They could then take up and pass any resolutions on the table. A safer and fairer procedure, however, would be to make an Objection to the Consideration of the Question (Section 15). This would assume that the matter is so objectionable that it would be best not to allow even its introducer to speak on it. But if there already had been debate on the subject, you couldn't object to its consideration. You could, however, make a motion for the Previous Question (Section 20); if that motion would pass, it immediately would bring the assembly to a vote. These motions are all legitimate ways of finding out if a group really wants to discuss a subject. Since the motions require a two-thirds vote, no one should object to them.

The motion to Lay [a question] on the Table can't be applied to more than the matter that's before the assembly at the time and whatever properly pertains to it. Therefore, it would be improper to lay aside committee reports (two or more) or unfinished business in general (all of the applicable subjects) when that part of the meeting is reached. Possible alternatives would be to move to Suspend the Rules (Section 18), a motion that requires a two-thirds vote, or to Lay on the Table each successive, *individual* report as it comes up for action.

Section 20. The Previous Question

The *Previous Question* is a technical name for a motion that gives one the wrong impression. It has nothing to do with the subject considered previously. To demand the Previous Question is to move that debate cease and the assembly immediately vote on the *pending* question(s). Therefore, when the chair asks, "Shall the main question be now put [to a vote]?" he or she really means, "Shall the *pending* question be now put [to a vote]?" (See Section 37 for the motion to Limit Debate.)

The Previous Question, which is not debatable, takes precedence over every debatable question (see Section 35). But it yields to incidental questions (see Section 8) and privileged questions (see Section 9) and to the motion to Lay on the Table (Section 19). After someone demands the Previous Question and until final action on it is taken, you may move to Adjourn (Section 11) or move that the main question be laid on the table.

The Previous Question can't be amended or have any other subsidiary motion (see Section 7) applied to it. But *it* can be applied to, or used together with, Questions of Privilege (Section 12) as well as to any other debatable question; you could, therefore, submit a resolution and at the same time move for the Previous Question.

The Previous Question may be reconsidered but not after being partially executed. To be adopted, it requires a two-thirds vote. A single vote is taken in reconsidering the Previous Question. The chair would ask:

Will the assembly reconsider the motion ordering the Previous Question?

If the vote is in favor of reconsidering it, the main question is free of the Previous Question. Since the Previous Question is itself undebatable and also ends the debate on the main question, members wouldn't vote to reconsider it unless they wanted to reopen the debate.

In the House the motion for the Previous Question must be seconded by a majority (to avoid the "yeas and nays" [see Section 38]), and then it can be adopted by a majority vote; in the Senate this is not allowed. In the House the motion is sometimes called the "gag law" since a bare majority can adopt it. The right of debate, however, should be considered an established rule in every deliberative body, one that can't be changed except by a vote that can suspend any rule (see Section 39).

When someone calls for the Previous Question, and the call is seconded, the chair immediately asks a question such as one of the following:

Shall the main question be now put?
Are you ready for the question?

A vote is then taken on the Previous Question, and if the motion fails, the discussion on the original subject (main question) continues as though the motion calling for the Previous Question had never been made. If the motion passes, though, its effect is as follows:

- The effect of passing a call for the Previous Question (except when motions to Amend and to Commit are pending) is to close the debate instantly and to require that the assembly vote on the pending question. (But after the debate is closed on a question reported from a committee, the person reporting it may make a closing speech. See Section 34.) After the assembly has voted, the business before the assembly stands exactly as if the vote on the pending motion had been taken in the usual way (without a demand for the Previous Question having forced the vote). If the vote on the Previous Question is reconsidered (see Section 27), the matter (main question) is released from the Previous Question and is again open to debate.

- The effect when either of the motions to Amend (Section 23) or to Commit (Section 22) is pending is to cut off debate and force a vote not only on those motions but also on the main question to be amended or committed. If you think of the motions to Amend and to Commit as inseparable from the main question to be amended or committed, there is really only one question. Then the effect of adopting the Previous Question is simply to cut off debate and force the assembly to vote on that one pending question. This may be the easiest way to view this matter since it makes it as simple as adopting an order closing debate (see Section 37). The motion to Close Debate would have the same privileges (and therefore the same complications) as the Previous Question.

The chair puts to a vote these various motions in order of precedence, beginning with the motion that was made last. The Previous Question is not exhausted (concluded) until votes have been taken on all of the pending questions (to Amend, to Commit, and so on) or until there has been a vote to refer the matter to a committee. If one of the votes is reconsidered before the Previous Question is exhausted, the fact that the Previous Question is pending means that the motion being reconsidered can't be debated.

The motion for the Previous Question may be limited to or concern only the pending amendment; if the motion passes, then, debate is closed only on the amendment. After the amendment is voted on, the main question (the one that was being amended) is again open to debate and further amendment. Acceptable forms of the question are as follows:

Shall the question be now put on the amendment?
Shall the debate close now and a vote be taken on the amendment?

In the same manner, you can make a motion to amend an amendment.

The object of the Previous Question is to bring the assembly to an immediate vote on the subject being considered without further debate. For other ways of closing debate, see Sections 37 and 38.

An Appeal (Section 14) from the decision of the chair is undebatable (see Section 35) if it's made after someone has moved for the Previous Question and before final action is taken.

The following examples illustrate the effect of the Previous Question in various circumstances:

Example: Suppose that a question is before the assembly and someone makes a motion to Amend it. Then imagine that someone else moves to Postpone [the question] to a Certain Time (Section 21). If the Previous Question is ordered, it stops the debate and forces a vote on the pending question—the postponement. When that vote is taken, the effect of the Previous Question is exhausted (no longer applies). But if the assembly refuses to postpone the subject, the debate on the pending amendment is resumed.

Example: Suppose that the subject under consideration is interrupted by a Question of Privilege (Section 12) and that someone moves to refer the Question of Privilege to a committee. If the Previous Question is ordered, it brings the assembly to a vote, first on the motion to Commit and, if that one fails, next on the Question of Privilege. After the Question of Privilege is voted on, the Previous Question is exhausted, so consideration of the subject is resumed.

Example: Suppose that while an amendment to a question is pending someone makes a motion to refer the matter to a committee. Then someone moves to Amend the referral motion by giving the committee instructions. In addition to the main question, therefore, two other motions have been made—to Amend and to Commit. If someone calls for the Previous Question, it will apply to all of the motions as though there is just one question. The chair will immediately put the question to a vote:

- First, on the committee's instructions.

- Second, on the motion to Commit; if this is adopted the subject is referred to the committee, and the effect of the Previous Question is exhausted.

- Third, if the motion to Commit fails, on the amendment.

- Finally, on the main question.

Much of the confusion about the Previous Question has been caused by the great changes in this motion since its conception in the English Parliament. There it was intended and is still used to suppress the main question (not the debate). It was first used in 1604 and was intended to be applied only to delicate questions. The form then was "Shall the main question be put?" If there was a negative response the main question was dismissed for that session. The present form is "Shall the main question be now put?" At first, if the response was negative the question was dismissed only until after the ensuing debate. Now it's dismissed for the day. The motion for the Previous Question could be debated, but once it was voted on, it prevented any discussion of the main question. If the vote was yes (to "put" the main question), the main question was immediately put to a vote. If the vote was no (not to "put" the main question), the main question was dismissed for the day.

Congress has changed the idea of the Previous Question. Whereas in England the one who moves for the Previous Question votes against it, in the United States the mover votes for it. In 1805 Congress made the Previous Question undebatable. In 1860 Congress allowed the consideration of a subject to be resumed if the Previous Question didn't pass. At first its effect was to cut off all motions except the main question, and a vote was immediately taken on it. In 1840 this was changed to bring the House to a vote first on pending amendments and then on the main question. In 1848 the rule was changed again to bring the House to a vote on the motion to Commit (if any), then on amendments reported by a committee (if any), next on pending amendments, and finally on the main question. In 1860 Congress decided that the only effect of the Previous Question, if a motion to postpone were pending, should be to bring the House to a direct vote on the postponement. This would prevent the Previous Question from cutting off any pending motion. The Previous Question is now a simple motion to close debate and proceed to voting. (But to stop someone from introducing an improper or useless subject in an ordinary assembly, one should object to its consideration [see Section 15] when first introduced. This motion is very similar to the English Previous Question.)

Section 21. To Postpone to a Certain Time

The motion to Postpone to a Certain Time a particular question takes precedence over a motion to Commit (Section 22) or Amend (Section 23) or Postpone Indefinitely (Section 24). But it yields to any incidental question (see Section 8) or privileged question (see Section 9) and to the motion to Lay on the Table (Section 19) or to a call for the Previous Question (Section 20). It can be amended by altering the time, and the Previous Question can be applied to the motion to Postpone without affecting any other pending motions. It allows very limited debate (see Section 35); such debate, however, must not delve into the merits of the subject any more than is necessary for the assembly to make a judgment about postponement.

The effect of the motion to Postpone to a Certain Time is to postpone the entire subject to a specified time. Until that time it can't be taken up unless there's a two-thirds vote (see Section 13) to do so. When the specified time arrives, it may be taken up in preference to everything else except privileged questions (Section 9). When several questions are postponed to different times but are not brought up at those times, the subjects eventually must be considered in the order of the times to which they were postponed. If you propose another time, it may not be beyond the *current* session of the assembly (see Section 42). It may, however, be postponed to the next *regular* session, at which time the subject would come up with the unfinished business and thus would take precedence over new business on that day (see Section 44). If members want to hold an adjourned meeting to consider a special subject, someone should move to Fix the Time to Which to Adjourn (Section 10) before making a motion to postpone the subject to that day. (In Congress a motion can't be postponed to the next session, although it is customary in ordinary societies to do this.)

Section 22. To Commit or Refer

The motion to Commit or Refer a subject to a committee takes precedence over the motions to Amend (Section 23) or to Postpone Indefinitely (Section 24). (When a subject was previously committed, the proper term is to *Recommit*.) But the motion yields to any incidental question (see Section 8) or any privileged question (see Section 9). It also yields to the motions to Lay on the Table (Section 19), to a call for the Previous Question (Section 20), and to Postpone to a Certain Time (Section 21). It can be amended by altering the committee or giving the committee instructions. The motion is debatable, and it opens to debate (see Section 35) the merits of the question to be committed.

The form of the motion is as follows:

I move to refer ____ to a committee.

When different committees are proposed, they should be voted on in the following order:

• Committee of the whole (see Section 32)

• Standing committee

• Special (or select) committee

The number of a committee is usually decided without the formality of a motion, as is the case in filling in blanks (see Section 23). The chair would ask something similar to these examples:

Of how many shall the committee consist?
How many shall there be on the committee?

A motion is then made for each number suggested, starting with the smallest number. But the number of members and kind of committee need not be decided until after the vote to refer the subject to a committee has taken place.

With a select committee, when the motion does not state how to appoint it and there is no standing rule on the subject, the chair will ask how the committee should be appointed. This matter is usually decided informally. Sometimes the chair appoints the members, simply naming them without any vote on them. The committee could also be nominated by the chair or members of the assembly. No one, however, should nominate more than one person except by general consent. Then the nominees are all voted on together unless there are more people nominated than the number proposed for the committee; in that case, each one would have to be voted on individually.

A committee formed for some activity (such as making arrangements for a building dedication) generally should be small. Also, no one should be on it who is opposed to the proposed action. Any opponent who is appointed should ask to be excused. A committee formed for purposes of investigation or deliberation, though, must have all parties (that is, those representing all sides of an issue) on it to provide for thorough discussion in the committee and to avoid later unpleasant debates in the assembly. In ordinary assemblies the careful selection of committee members representing all views of delicate and troublesome questions will help to limit debates to the committee itself (see Section 28).

Section 23. To Amend

The motion to Amend another motion takes precedence only over the motion to be amended. It yields to any other subsidiary motion (see Section 7) except one to Postpone [a matter] Indefinitely (Section 24), any incidental motion (see Section 8), or any privileged motion (see Section 9). It can be applied to all motions except the eight motions listed later in this section, which can't be amended. The motion to Amend can itself even be amended, although such amendment of an amendment can't be altered further.

An amendment could be inconsistent with another one already adopted, and it also could be in direct conflict with the spirit of the original motion. But it must have a direct bearing on the subject of the original motion.

> *Example:* A motion for a vote of thanks could be amended by striking out *thanks* and inserting the word *censure.*

> *Example:* A motion condemning certain customs could be amended by adding other customs.

An amendment may take any of the following forms:

- To "add" or "insert" certain words or paragraphs.

- To "strike out" certain words or paragraphs. If that motion fails to pass, another amendment is possible. (Previously, the form for this motion was "Shall these words stand as part of the resolution?" Now, in the United States, it's treated the same as any other motion.)

- To "strike out certain words and insert others." This motion can't be divided. If it fails to pass, another one can be offered to strike out the same words and insert different words. (Rule 18 of the Senate states that in amending a motion to strike out A and insert B, the amendment is considered as two questions, and the amendment to the first part on words to be removed takes precedence.)

- To "substitute" another resolution or paragraph on the same subject for the one that's pending.

- To "divide the question" into two or more motions, as the mover specifies, to get a separate vote on some point(s) (see Section 4).

If you want to insert a paragraph, it should be worded exactly as the proponents want it to read—*before* voting on it. Once it has been inserted, it's too late: It can't be struck out or amended, except by adding to it. The same thing is true concerning words to be inserted in a resolution. Once they're inserted, they can't be taken out except by making a motion to strike out (1) the entire paragraph or (2) some portion of it that would make the motion entirely different from what it would be with the words inserted. In other words, once a group has voted to insert certain words in a resolution, it's not in order to make another motion involving exactly the same question that was just decided. The only way to bring it up again is to move to Reconsider (Section 27) the vote that was taken to insert the words.

Filling Blanks. Amendments about filling in blanks differ from others in that members may propose, without a second, different numbers for filling in the blank(s). These proposals, however, are not treated as amendments of one another; they're considered to be independent propositions that must be voted on successively. The correct order for voting is that the smallest sum and the longest time are put first. (The Senate follows this practice of not treating the proposals as amendments of one another and also gives preference to the smallest sum. The House, though, treats filling in blanks the same as other amendments.)

Nominations. As is the case with filling in blanks, with nominations a second nomination is not considered to be an amendment of the first; rather, it's an independent motion to be voted on if the first one fails to receive a majority vote.

Any number of nominations may be made, and the chair should announce each name as it's given. The nominations should then be voted on in the order announced by the chair until someone is elected. This requires a majority vote unless the organization's bylaws specify a different number.

If paragraphs in an amendment are numbered, the numbers are treated as merely marginal notations, not part of the paragraph content. They should be corrected (if necessary), therefore, by the clerk without making any motion to Amend (to correct the number).

Amending an organization's rules of order, bylaws, or constitution would require first giving previous notice to the members and then a two-thirds vote for the amendment to pass (see Section 45; for instructions on amending the reports of committees or propositions with several paragraphs, see Section 31; on amending the minutes of meetings, see Section 41; on the proper form for making a motion to Amend, see Section 65.)

These motions can't be amended:

- To Adjourn, when unqualified (Section 11)
- For the Orders of the Day (Section 13)
- All incidental questions (Section 8)
- To Lay on the Table (Section 19)
- For the Previous Question (Section 20)
- To Amend an Amendment (Section 23)
- To Postpone Indefinitely (Section 24)
- To Reconsider (Section 27)

The following guidelines apply to amendments:

- A resolution is amended by altering the words of the resolution.

- An amendment is amended by altering the words of the amendment—that is, by altering the words to be inserted or taken out.

- The *form* of a motion to Amend can't be amended; that is, a motion to adopt a resolution can't be amended to substitute a motion to reject the resolution (that would alter the form, not the words, of the resolution). For example:

- A motion to "strike out A" can't be amended by adding "and insert B" (which would be read as "strike out A and insert B"); that would be another form of amendment and not an alteration of A.

- A motion to "insert B before the word C" in a resolution can't be amended by substituting another resolution for the one pending, thus changing the form of the amendment and not simply altering B.

- A motion to "insert B before the word C" can't be amended by adding "and D before the word E"; the only thing that can be altered in the pending amendment is B; the other words are those that are necessary to describe what is being proposed to do with B.

- If a pending amendment is to "insert A, B, C, and D before F," it's in order to apply any form of amendment to A, B, C, and D. But no amendment is in order that's not confined simply to altering the words A, B, C, and D.

- When a member wants to make a motion for an amendment that's not in order at the time but affects the pending question, that person should state his or her intention to offer another amendment if the pending amendment is voted down. Then those who favor that member's alternative amendment have a chance to vote down the pending amendment, paving the way for the new one to be offered.

Section 24. To Postpone Indefinitely

The motion to Postpone [a subject] Indefinitely takes precedence only over the principal question (see Section

6). It yields to any other subsidiary motion (see Section 7) except to Amend (Section 23), any incidental motion (see Section 8), or any privileged motion (see Section 9). It can be applied only to a principal question or a Question of Privilege (Section 12). The motion to Postpone Indefinitely can't be amended. It opens to debate the entire question proposed for postponement. If the Previous Question (Section 20) is ordered when the motion to Postpone Indefinitely is pending, the Previous Question applies to it alone and doesn't affect the main question.

The effect of a motion to Postpone Indefinitely is to remove the question from the assembly for that session (see Section 42). A vote to Postpone Indefinitely is the same as a negative vote on the main question. But it's useful when the opposition doubts its strength. Even if opponents are defeated on the matter of postponement, then, they still will have a chance to fight the main question.

Miscellaneous Motions

Section 25. To Rescind

The motion to Rescind is used when an assembly wants to annul some prior action and it's too late to reconsider (see Section 27) the vote. This motion has no privileges but has the same importance as a new resolution. Any action of a group can be rescinded regardless of the time that has elapsed.

In rare cases, when a group wants not only to rescind some action but to express very strong disapproval, it could vote to rescind the objectionable resolution and remove it from the record. You would do this by crossing out the words, or drawing a line around them, and writing across the words "Expunged by order of the assembly . . . ," adding the date of the order.

Section 26. Renewal of a Motion

Once a principal question (see Section 6) or amendment has been acted on by a group, it can't be taken up again at the same session (see Section 42) except by making a motion to Reconsider (Section 27) the vote on it. Moreover, once that motion to Reconsider has been acted on, it, too, can't be repeated in regard to the same question—unless the question was amended when it was previously reconsidered. But a correction of the minutes (see Section 41) can be made without a motion to Reconsider at the same or any subsequent session. A motion to Rescind (Section 25) can also be made at the same or any subsequent session. The motion to Adjourn (Section 11) can be renewed if in the meantime the debate has progressed or if any business has since been transacted.

Generally, if any motion is introduced that alters the state of affairs, this means that you can renew (1) any privileged or incidental motion (except for a motion calling for Orders of the Day [Section 13] or to Suspend the Rules [Section 18]) or (2) any subsidiary motion (except for an amendment). The reason that it's possible to renew such motions is that the real question before the assembly is then different.

> *Example:* Suppose that a motion for a subject to Lay on the Table (Section 19) fails and someone then moves to Refer (Section 22) the matter to a committee. It would then be in order to move again that the subject lie on the table. Such a motion would not be in order, though, if you waited until the motion to Refer failed. If it failed, the question would return to its previous status. Therefore, if a subject has been taken from the table or if an objection to considering it has been voted down, you can't move to Lay it on the Table because that would involve essentially the same question that the assembly just decided.

When a subject has been referred to a committee that reports at the *same* meeting, the matter is then treated as if it has been introduced for the first time. Also, a motion that has been withdrawn in a meeting obviously hasn't been acted on, so it can then be renewed.

Section 27. To Reconsider

You may move to Reconsider a vote and have the motion entered on the record at any time—except while another question is before the assembly—including (1) when someone else has the floor, (2) while the assembly is voting on a motion to Adjourn (Section 11), (3) during the day when the motion of concern has been acted on, or (4) on the next succeeding day. But if the vote on some motion isn't reconsidered on the day it was taken and if no meeting is held the next day, it can't be reconsidered at the next meeting. The proper course then would be to renew the motion if it previously failed or to Rescind (Section 25) it if it was previously adopted.

The motion to Reconsider a vote must be made by a member who voted with the prevailing side (whether it was for or against), unless the vote was by ballot, in which case votes are secret. Anyone can second the motion. (In Congress anyone can move to Reconsider unless the vote was taken by "yeas and nays" [Section 38], in which case the above rule applies.) If a motion fails to pass for lack of a two-thirds vote, the move to Reconsider must be made by the person who voted against the motion—in this case, someone who voted against it would be on the prevailing side.

A motion to Reconsider the vote on a subsidiary question (see Section 7) takes precedence over the main question. But it yields to incidental questions (see Section 8) and privileged questions (see Section 9) except for the Orders of the Day.

The motion to Reconsider can be applied to the vote on every other question except one to Adjourn (Section 11) or to Suspend the Rules (Section 18) and except for an affirmative vote on the motion to Lay [a matter] on the Table or to Take [a matter] from the Table (Section 19) as well as a vote electing someone to office who is present and doesn't decline. One should not reconsider an affirmative vote on the motion to Lay on the Table because the same results can be obtained by making a motion to Take from the Table. For the same reason one wouldn't reconsider an affirmative vote to Take from the Table.

No question may be reconsidered twice unless it was amended after reconsidering it the first time. The minutes, however, may be corrected any number of times without making a motion to Reconsider the vote approving them. If an amendment to a motion has been adopted (or rejected) and then if a vote is taken on the motion as amended, you may not reconsider the vote on the amendment until you have first reconsidered the vote on the original motion. Also, if the Previous Question (Section 20) has been partially executed, it may not be reconsidered, either.

If there is something that an assembly can't reverse— something that was done by vote—that vote can't be reconsidered. A motion to Reconsider a vote can't be amended. It may or may not be debated, depending on whether the question that's being reconsidered may or may not be debated (see Section 35). When a motion to Reconsider is debatable, it also opens to discussion the entire subject that's being reconsidered. But if the Previous Question (Section 20) is ordered while a motion to Reconsider is pending, the Previous Question affects only the motion to Reconsider, not the entire subject being reconsidered.

The motion to Reconsider can itself be laid on the table (see Section 19), in which case the reconsideration, like any other question that was set aside, can later be taken from the table. But it has no privileges. When a motion to Reconsider is laid on the table, it doesn't carry with it the pending measure (the one being reconsidered).

The effect of making a motion to Reconsider is to suspend all action that would have been necessary under the original motion until the members act on the recon-

In Congress a member in charge of an important bill usually moves to Reconsider the vote on it as soon as it passes. At the same time the member usually moves that the motion to Reconsider be laid on the table. If the motion to Lay [the reconsideration] on the Table is adopted, the decision is considered final, since the large number of bills awaiting action means that it will not likely be taken up again, except by a two-thirds vote. This isn't true in ordinary societies, however, and there is no good reason in this case to violate the principle that only one motion can be made at a time.

sideration. But (with one exception) if the motion to Reconsider is not called up for action (a vote) during the session, its effect terminates with *that* session (see Section 42). An exception applies to an assembly having regular meetings as often as monthly when there's no adjourned meeting (of the meeting at which the move was made to Reconsider) held on another day. Then the effect of making the motion to Reconsider does not end until the close of the *next* succeeding session. The move to Reconsider a subsidiary motion (see Section 7) or an incidental motion (see Section 8) must be acted on immediately, since otherwise the members couldn't act on the main question. An exception occurs when the vote to be reconsidered had the effect of removing the entire subject before the assembly.

Example: Suppose that a motion to Postpone Indefinitely is voted down, indicating that the group wants to consider the subject in question. If someone moves to Reconsider that last vote, the reconsideration has to be acted on immediately, as explained above, or, in effect, the whole subject will be removed, without any possible benefit to the assembly. If you want to stop a temporary majority from adopting a resolution, the proper course is to wait until the assembly finally acts on the resolution and then move to Reconsider

the vote on it. But suppose that a motion to
Postpone Indefinitely passes; then the subject is
removed from before the assembly. In that case
the reconsideration can be held over to another
day and other business can be transacted in the
meantime.

Although the motion to Reconsider is very highly privileged in regard to having it entered in the minutes (with
action on it delayed until it is called up later), the reconsideration of another matter must not interfere with the
discussion of a subject before the assembly. As soon as
that subject is disposed of, however, the reconsideration,
if called up, takes precedence over everything except the
motions to Adjourn (Section 11) and to Fix the Time to
Which to Adjourn (Section 10). When a reconsideration
has been called up (brought before the assembly for
action), it can be treated like any other motion and can
be held over as unfinished business. As long as the effect
of the reconsideration lasts (that is, it hasn't yet been
disposed of), anyone may call up the motion to Reconsider and have it acted on. An exception to this is when
its effect extends beyond the meeting at which the motion to Reconsider was made; then no one but the mover
can call it up at that meeting.

The effect of adopting the motion to Reconsider is to
put the original question before the assembly in the exact
position it held before it was voted on. Hence no one can
debate the question to be reconsidered who previously
has exhausted his or her right to debate (see Section 34)
that question. A person's only recourse, then, is to discuss the question while the motion to Reconsider is before the assembly.

When a vote taken under the order of the Previous
Question (Section 20) is reconsidered, the original question is then free of the Previous Question and is again
open to debate and amendment. This is true as long as
the Previous Question was acted on (exhausted)—by votes
taken on all of the subjects it concerned—before the
motion to Reconsider was made.

A reconsideration needs only a majority vote. This is

In the English Parliament, once a vote is taken, it can't be reconsidered. But in the U.S. Congress, members may move to Reconsider a vote on the same or the succeeding day. After the close of the last day for making the motion, anyone may call up the motion to Reconsider. Therefore, this motion can't delay action more than two days, and the effect of the motion, if not acted on, terminates with the session. There seems to be no reason or good precedent for allowing two persons, by moving to Reconsider, to suspend for any length of time all action under resolutions adopted by the assembly. Yet when the delay is very short, the advantages of reconsideration outweigh the disadvantages.

When a permanent society has weekly or monthly meetings and when, usually, only a small percentage of the members are present, it seems best to permit a reconsideration to hold over to another meeting so that a larger proportion of the group will be aware of what action is about to be taken.

Steps can be taken to prevent someone from using the motion to Reconsider a vote to defeat a measure that can't be deferred until the next regular meeting; in case the society adjourns until another day, the reconsideration will not hold over beyond that session. This allows sufficient delay to notify the society about the motion; if the question requires immediate action, the delay can't extend beyond the day to which the meeting adjourns. The rule is that the meeting must be held on another day to prevent the defeat of the whole object of the reconsideration by an immediate adjournment merely until a few minutes later.

When meetings are only quarterly or annual, a society should be properly represented at each meeting. The group's best interests are served by following the practice of Congress and letting the effect of the reconsideration end with the session.

true regardless of the vote needed (such as two-thirds) to adopt the motion that was reconsidered. (For reconsidering a vote in committee, see Section 28.)

Article IV. Committees and Informal Action

Section 28. Committees

Deliberative assemblies usually have committees do the preliminary work of preparing some matter for their action. These committees may be standing or select committees or committees of the whole (see Section 32). *Standing committees* are appointed for a particular session (see Section 42) or for some definite time such as one year. *Select committees* are appointed for a special purpose. *Committees of the whole* consist of the entire assembly. (For the method of appointing committees of the whole, see Section 32; for other committees, see Section 22.) A committee (except a committee of the whole; see Section 32) in turn may appoint a subcommittee.

The first person named to be on a committee is the committee chair. In the absence of that person, the next-named member becomes the committee chair and so on. The committee, however, has the authority to elect another chair if it wishes, unless the assembly has already appointed a committee chair. The clerk of the assembly should advise the committee chair, or another member of the committee, of the appointment of the committee and give (1) the names of the members, (2) the matter referred to them, and (3) any instructions from the assembly.

An *ex-officio member* of a committee or board is a member by virtue of holding some office. But if the office isn't controlled by the society, there's no distinction between the ex-officio member and other members. If the ex-officio member is *not* under the authority of the organization, he or she has all of the privileges but none of the obligations of membership. This is similar to the status of a governor of a state who is acting ex-officio as manager or trustee of a private academy. Sometimes the bylaws specify that the group's president shall be ex-officio a member of every committee. The intent in such cases is to *allow,* not require, the president to act as a member of the various committees. In determining a quorum, then, the president should not be counted as a member of the committee. The president would be a member of any committee only by virtue of a special rule, unless the assembly would appoint him or her as a member.

Once the committee is formed, its chair should call the members together. If there's a quorum (a majority; see Section 43), the chair would then read, or have read, the entire resolution(s) referred to the committee. After reading each paragraph, the chair should pause to allow amendments to be offered. After any amendments to a particular paragraph are voted on, the chair would read the next paragraph and so on. The committee can only vote on amendments; it can't vote to adopt the matter referred by the assembly.

The resolutions, however, might originate in a committee rather than the assembly. There they would be prepared by a committee member(s) or a subcommittee. Nevertheless, the committee would still handle the draft of any resolution paragraph by paragraph and vote on amendments in the same manner. The vote on each paragraph would concern amendments only, however; the committee would not vote to adopt each paragraph. Rather, at the end of all votes on amendments, it would vote to adopt the entire report (see Section 31). A preamble (if any) is considered last. When the report originates in a committee, all amendments are incorporated into the report. But when resolutions are referred to a committee by the assembly, the committee must not alter the text. Instead, it must submit to the assembly the original paper intact with the committee's amendments (which may be in the form of a substitute such as other resolutions or paragraphs; see Section 23) written on a separate sheet of paper.

A committee is a miniature assembly that must meet to

transact business. Any two members can call for a meeting if the committee chair is absent or declines to call a meeting. Usually, one of the members is appointed as clerk, or secretary. When a quorum is present, a majority of the members at the meeting must agree in order for something to form part of the committee's report. The minority, however, may submit its views in writing (together or each member separately). But minority reports can be acted on only by voting to substitute one of them for the report of the committee (see Section 30).

The rules of the assembly, as much as possible, apply in committee. The committee chair usually takes the most active part in the discussions and work. A motion, however, does not require a second, and (except in large committees) a member does not have to stand while speaking. Although small committees may dispense with motions, they should always take a vote to establish exactly what has been decided. A reconsideration (see Section 27) of a vote is allowed, regardless of the time elapsed, only when every member who voted with the majority is present when someone moves to Reconsider the vote.

Both English common parliamentary law and the rules of Congress prohibit a committee from reconsidering a vote. But if this rule were strictly enforced in ordinary committees it would hinder rather than help efforts to transact business. The rule allowing a reconsideration seems more just and appropriate for ordinary committees. The privilege won't be abused as long as everyone who voted with the majority is present when the move to Reconsider occurs.

When a committee is finished with the business assigned to it, someone makes a motion for the committee to Rise and for the chair (or another member more familiar with the subject) to report to the assembly. In a committee, the motion to Rise is the same as the motion to Adjourn (Section 11) in an assembly. As soon as the assembly receives the report (see Section 30), the committee ceases to exist, unless it's a standing committee.

A committee has no power to punish its members for disorderly conduct, but it can report the pertinent facts to the assembly. It can't, however, allude to what has occurred except by a report of the committee to the assembly or by general consent.

When a committee adjourns without setting a time for the next meeting, it's called together in the same way as occurred at its first meeting. When a committee adjourns to meet at another time, it's not necessary (but is a good idea) to notify absent members of the adjourned meeting.

Section 29. Forms of Committee Reports

The usual form of introducing a report is illustrated in these examples:

Standing Committee: **The committee on ____ respectfully reports [*or* "respectfully submits the following report"] . . . [*followed by the report comments*].**

Select or Special Committee: **The committee [*or* "Your committee" *or* "The undersigned, a committee"] to which was referred ____, having considered the same, respectfully reports . . . [*followed by the report comments*].**

Minority Report: **The undersigned, a minority of a committee to which we referred, . . . [*followed by the report comments*].**

Unlike the minority report, the majority report is the report of the committee and should not be described as the report of the majority.

A report may conclude by stating something such as the following examples:

All of which is respectfully submitted.

Respectfully submitted.

But this is not necessary. It usually is signed only by the chair of the committee. If the matter is of great importance, however, it should be signed by every member who concurs in the report. Although a report is not usually dated or addressed, it may have a heading such as this:

Report of the Finance Committee of the YPA on Renting a Hall

The report would usually close or be accompanied by a formal resolution covering all of its recommendations. The adoption of the report (see Section 31) would then have the effect of adopting all of the resolutions necessary to carry out the committee's recommendations. The following example, however, illustrates an exception to this effect:

Example: Suppose that a committee report on a certain subject also stated: "Your committee thinks that the conduct of Mrs. Mulligan at the last meeting was so disgraceful that it recommends that she be expelled from the society." The adoption of the committee's report by the governing assembly would not have the effect of expelling Mrs. Mulligan.

A committee may be able to carry out its assigned task just by reporting a resolution. In that case, the resolution alone is submitted in writing.

Section 30. Reception of Reports

When a committee is ready to report, the committee chair or someone appointed to make the report informs the assembly. The person selected would indicate to the assembly that the committee to which a particular subject or paper was referred had directed him or her to report thereon or to report it with or without amendment, as the case may be. That person or another member might then move that the report be received at the time or at another specified time.

Sometimes errors in procedure occur at this stage, as shown in these examples:

> *Example:* A very common error occurs after a report has been read. Someone may move that the report be *received* then. But the fact that it has been read indicates that the assembly has already received it.

> *Example:* A less common but dangerous mistake concerns the adoption of a report. A group may vote to *accept* a report (equivalent to adopting it; see Section 31) when it means only to consider the report and, after that, move for adoption.

> *Example:* Another error involves the discharge of a committee. Someone may move that "the report be adopted and *the committee be discharged*" when the committee has already reported in full and its report has already been received. By that time, therefore, the committee no longer exists anyway. On the other hand, if the committee had made only a partial report or a progress report, it would be in order to move to discharge the committee from further consideration of the subject.

Usually, an assembly dispenses with the formality of a vote to receive a committee report, and the time when the report will be given is settled be general consent. But if anyone objects, a formal motion is necessary. When it's time for the assembly to receive the report, the chair of the committee (or other members) reads it (without leaving his or her seat) before delivering it to the clerk of the assembly. It will then lie on the table (see Section 19) until the assembly is ready to consider it. But after the committee chair (or other person) reads the report, it's a good idea for him or her to move that the assembly accept (or adopt) it or to make whatever other motion will carry out the committee's recommendations.

If a report consists of a paper with amendments, the committee chair (or other person) would read the amendments along with enough of the related part in the paper to be understandable. The person reading would explain the alterations and give reasons for the amendments as each one came up until he or she had gone through all of them. When a report is very long, it's usually read when the assembly is ready to consider it (see Section 31).

Once a report has been received, whether or not it has been read, the committee is thereby dissolved and can act no further unless there's a vote to Recommit the matter (send it back to the committee). If the report is recommitted, all parts not agreed to by the assembly are ignored by the committee as though the report had never been made.

If a member(s) wants to submit a minority report(s), the assembly usually receives it right after receiving the committee report. But the assembly can't act on the minority report unless someone moves to substitute it for the committee report.

Section 31. Adoption of Reports

When an assembly is ready to consider a report, someone should move to *adopt, accept,* or *agree to* the report. You can use any of those terms to accomplish the same thing. When the motion is carried, they all have the effect of making the committee's work become the acts of the assembly just as if the assembly had done the work without a committee. Therefore, if the committee's report has formal resolutions, the assembly adopts those resolutions. (But when a committee's report is only informational, there is no need to take any action after it has been read.)

The motions to adopt, accept, or agree to a report generally are used indiscriminately. But even though they all have the same effect, it would be better to vary the motion according to the character of the report.

> *Example:* Suppose that the report contains only a statement of opinion or facts. The best form, then, is to *accept* the report.

> *Example:* Suppose that the report contains a statement of opinion and facts but also concludes with resolutions or orders. The best form, then, is to *agree to* the resolution or to *adopt* the orders. If either of these motions is carried, the effect is to adopt the entire report.

To *adopt* the report is the most common of the motions in ordinary societies; it's used regardless of the character of the report. Although the effect of the motion to adopt a report is generally understood, that's not always the case with the term *to accept*. (See Section 30; see also Section 30 for common errors in acting on reports; see Section 29 for the way in which the form of a report influences its adoption.)

After someone moves either to accept or to adopt a report, the report is open to amendment. The matter then stands before the assembly as if there had been no committee and as if the subject had just been introduced by the motion of the member who was reporting.

One should be especially careful with an annual report of an executive committee or board of managers that's published as its report. The assembly should be careful in amending it to show clearly what the board is responsible for and what pertains to the society. As a precaution, one could prefix to the report a statement such as this:

> The report was adopted by the society after striking out what is enclosed in brackets and adding what is printed in footnotes.

When a committee reports on a resolution that was referred to it by the assembly, the assembly's presiding officer should state the question, depending on the recommendation of the committee, as follows:

- If the committee recommends that the resolution be adopted or makes no recommendation, the question should be stated (by the chair) first on any pending amendment and then on the resolution. (Since these motions were pending when the matter was referred to the committee, they wouldn't be made again.)

- If the committee's recommendation is that the resolution not be adopted, the question should be stated on adopting (or not adopting) the resolution.

- If the committee recommends that the resolution be postponed indefinitely, or postponed to a certain time, the question should be stated on postponing indefinitely or to a certain time.

- If the committee recommends that the resolution be amended in a certain way, the question should be stated, first, on adopting the proposed amendment to the resolution and, then, on adopting the resolution itself.

In all of these cases, immediately after the committee's report is read, someone should make a motion as indicated above. The appropriate person to make it, if the committee makes any recommendation, is the committee member who reports to the assembly. If no one makes a motion, the assembly's chair should state the proper motion and ask if someone will make it. If the proper motion has already been made, the chair should immediately state the question (see Section 65).

A committee may submit a report that has a number of paragraphs or sections (such as a set of bylaws). In that case the entire paper should be read by the member reporting or by the clerk of the assembly. Then the member reporting or someone else should move to adopt it unless it was already done.

After the assembly's chair has stated the question on adopting the report, he or she should direct the member who reported or the assembly's clerk to read the first paragraph. *Paragraph* refers to a separate division of the proposition—for example, an article, a section, a paragraph, or a separate resolution.

No vote is taken on the adoption of each of the paragraphs; instead, upon completion, the entire paper is adopted. By not voting on the paragraphs one at a time, the assembly can go back after all have been amended and amend any of them further. In a committee, a similar paper would be treated the same way (see Section 28; see Section 48 for a practical example). Should each paragraph be adopted separately, it would be improper afterwards to vote on adopting the entire report. Similarly, it would be out of order to go back and amend a paragraph that was adopted until after it had been reconsidered.

After the first paragraph has been read to the assembly, the chair of the assembly should ask:

Are there any amendments proposed to this paragraph?

The chair should then pause for remarks or amendments, giving preference to the member who submitted the report if that person wants the floor. When satisfied that no one else wants the floor, the chair should state:

No (further) amendments being offered to this paragraph, the next will be read.

In this way each paragraph is read and amended. Then the chair states that the entire report, or all of the resolutions, have been read and are open to *further* amendment. At this stage new paragraphs may be inserted; even those originally in the report may be amended further since they have not yet been adopted. If there is a preamble, it should be read and amended after the body of the resolutions has been worded in final form. Then a vote is taken on adopting the entire report as amended.

When a committee reports back on a paper (that was referred to it) with committee amendments, the reporting member reads only the amendments and then makes a motion to adopt them. The chair states the question on the adoption of the amendments and asks for the first amendment to be read. After the reading, it's open to debate and further amendment by the assembly. A vote is then taken on adopting this amendment. After that, the next committee amendment is read and so on until all amendments are adopted or rejected. Only amendments to the committee's amendments are considered.

When the assembly is finished with the amendments, the chair of the assembly pauses for any further amendments to be proposed. When any such additional amendments are voted on, the chair "puts" the question on agreeing to or adopting the paper as amended (except in a case such as revising the bylaws since they have already been adopted).

By suspending the rules (see Section 18) or by general consent a report can be adopted at once without following any of the above routine. (See Section 34 for the privileges in debate of the member making the report to the assembly.)

Section 32. Committee of the Whole

Sometimes an assembly wants to consider a subject and does not want to refer it to a committee. The subject may not be well understood and may not be put into proper form for definite action. When in such cases it's desirable for an assembly to consider a subject with all of the freedom of an ordinary committee, the matter may be referred to a committee of the whole. In large assemblies such as the House of Representatives, where a member may speak only once on a question, a committee of the whole is almost a necessity. It allows the freest discussion of a subject and yet at any time it can "rise" (equivalent to adjourning in an assembly) and thus bring into force the strict rules of the assembly.

When a group wants to consider a question right away, someone should make a motion such as this:

I move that the assembly now resolve itself into a committee of the whole to consider _____.

This is really a motion to Commit (see Section 22 for its order of precedence). If the motion passes, the presiding officer of the assembly immediately calls another member to take over the chair, and then the presiding officer takes his or her place as a member of the committee of the whole.

A committee of the whole operates under the rules of the assembly except as indicated in this section. The only motions in order are those to Amend and to adopt and the motion that the committee "rise" and report, since it can't adjourn. Also, it can't order a vote by "yeas and nays" (see Section 38). (The only way to close or limit debate in a committee of the whole is for the assembly to vote [1] that the debate in committee will cease at a certain time or [2] that after a certain time no debate will be allowed except on new amendments. Even then, only one speech in favor of and one against, perhaps of five minutes each, will be allowed, or in some other way the time for debate will be regulated.)

In Congress no motion to limit debate in a committee of the whole is in order until after the subject has already been considered in the committee. Since probably no subject would be considered more than once in a committee of the whole, the enforcement of this rule in an ordinary society would practically prevent such a society from putting any limit to debate in the committee.

If no limit to debate is prescribed, any member may speak as often as he or she can get the floor. The member also may speak each time as long as the time allowed in debate in the assembly, provided that no one wants the floor who has not spoken on the question. If debate has been closed at a particular time by order of the assembly, the committee may not, even by unaminous consent, extend the time.

A committee of the whole may not refer a subject to another committee. Like other committees (see Section 28), it may not alter the text of any resolution referred to it. But if the resolution originated in the committee of the whole, all the amendments are incorporated in the resolution.

When a committee of the whole is through considering a subject referred to it or if it wants to adjourn or to have the assembly limit debate, someone should move that "the committee 'rise' and report," specifying the result of its proceedings. The motion to Rise, which is equivalent to the motion to Adjourn (Section 11) in the assembly, is always in order, except when another member has the floor, and can't be debated. As soon as this motion is adopted, the presiding officer returns to his or her place as chair of the assembly. The committee chair then returns to the assembly, rises (in a large or formal meeting), and informs the presiding officer that:

> **The committee has gone through the business referred to it. I'm ready to make the report when the assembly is ready to receive it.**

Or the committee chair may make such other report as is appropriate.

The assembly's clerk does not record the proceedings of the committee of the whole in the minutes but should keep a memo of the proceedings for the committee's use. In large meetings the clerk vacates his or her seat so that it can be occupied by the chair of the committee. The assistant clerk then acts as clerk of the committee.

If a committee of the whole becomes disorderly and the committee chair is unable to preserve order, the assembly's presiding officer can take back the chair and declare the committee dissolved. The quorum of the committee of the whole is the same as that of the assembly (see Section 43). If the committee should find itself without a quorum, though, it would have to report that fact to the assembly. In that case, the assembly would have to adjourn.

Section 33. Informal Consideration of a Question

Many assemblies, instead of going into a committee of the whole, consider a question informally; that is, they *act* as if they're in a committee of the whole. Then, afterwards, they take formal action. In a small assembly there's no objection to this.

> According to U.S. Senate Rules 28 and 38, all Senate bills, joint resolutions, and treaties, upon a second reading, are considered "as if the Senate were in a committee of the whole," which is equivalent to considering them informally. But in large assemblies it's better to follow the practice of the House and go into a committee of the whole.

While acting informally on any resolutions, the assembly can only amend and adopt them. Without any further motion the chair would then announce:

The assembly, acting informally [*or* "as in committee of the whole"], had ＿＿ subject under consideration and has made certain amendments that will be reported.

The subject comes before the assembly then as if reported by a committee. While acting informally, the chair retains his or her seat since it's not necessary to move that the committee "rise." But at any time, the informal consideration ends with the adoption of motions such as to Adjourn (Section 11), for the Previous Question (Section 20), and to Commit (Section 22), as well as any motion except to Amend (Section 23) or to adopt. For example, the motion to Commit is equivalent to the following motions when an assembly is acting as a committee of the whole:

- That the committee "rise"
- That the committee of the whole be discharged from further consideration of the subject
- That the question be referred to a committee

While an assembly is acting informally (as if in a committee of the whole), every member may speak as many times as desired and each time for as long as is allowed in the assembly (see Section 34). Also, the informal action may be rejected or altered by the assembly. The clerk should keep only a memo of the informal proceedings (not enter them in the minutes) since the information is only for temporary use. However, the chair's report to the assembly of the informal action should be entered in the minutes since it belongs to the assembly's proceedings.

Article V. Debate and Decorum

Section 34. Debate

When someone makes a motion and another member seconds it, the chair must state the question to the assembly before it's debated (read Sections 1–5 in connection with this section on debate). A member who wants to speak in debate should first rise (in a large or formal meeting) and respectfully address the chair:

Mr. Chairman
Madam Chairman

The title *Mr. President* or *Madame President* is used when that's the actual title of the presiding office. *Mr.* or *Madam Moderator* is more common in religious meetings. *Brother Moderator* is used in some parts of the country, although it implies an equality between the speaker and the chair that doesn't exist; only one is a moderator. Otherwise, a presiding officer should always be addressed by his or her official title.

After being addressed, the chair will announce the member's name (or show recognition in some other way). As a matter of parliamentary courtesy (or rule in the case of the U.S. House of Representatives), the member who has made a motion bringing some subject before the assembly is the one entitled to the floor first (see Section 2). This is true even when someone else rises first and addresses the chair. (With a committee report, the member who presents the report is entitled to the floor first). This person also is entitled to close the debate but only after everyone who wants to speak has had a chance to do so.

A member who reports a measure from a committee must be given the right to close the debate. Therefore, when someone calls for the Previous Question (see Section 20), the chair immediately assigns the floor to the reporting member to close the debate. Except for this practice allowing someone to open and close the debate, no one may speak more than twice on the same question and only once to a question of order (see Section 14). Also, no one may speak more than ten minutes at a time without permission from the assembly; the motion requesting this permission must be decided by a two-thirds vote (see Section 39) without debate. The time limit for debate would vary, though, to suit the circumstances. But a limit of two speeches of ten minutes each is usually appropriate in ordinary assemblies. If greater freedom is needed, the assembly could refer the matter in question to a committee of the whole (see Section 32) or consider

---

In the House no member may speak more than once on the same question or for more than one hour. The fourth rule of the Senate states: "No senator shall speak more than twice in any one debate, on the same day, without leave of the Senate, which question shall be decided without debate." If no such rule is adopted, each member can speak but once to the same question.

it informally (see Section 33). (On limiting or closing debate, see Section 37.)

No one may speak a second time on a question until every member who wants to speak has done so. Offering an amendment or making any other motion, however, changes the real question before the assembly to a different one. As far as debate is concerned, then, amendment is treated as a new question. Merely asking something or making a suggestion is not considered "speaking" on a question. Someone who makes a motion may vote against it but can't speak against the motion he or she made.

When an amendment is pending, the debate must be confined to the merits of that amendment. An exception to this rule would occur when the amendment is such that a decision on it practically decides the main question.

The chair can't close the debate as long as anyone wants to speak. If a member claims the floor *after* the chair has put the question to a vote or even after an affirmative vote has taken place—provided the negative has not been "put"—the member still has a right to resume the debate or make a motion.

Section 35. Undebatable Questions and Those That Open the Main Question to Debate

The following questions are decided without debate (all others are debatable):

- To Fix the Time to Which to Adjourn, when it's a privileged question (Section 10)

- To Adjourn or, in committee, to Rise (Section 11)

- For the Orders of the day (Section 13) and questions about the priority of business

- An Appeal (Section 14), when made while the Previous Question (Section 20) is pending or when simply relating to indecorum or transgressions of the rules of speaking or to the priority of business

• Objection to the Consideration of a Question (Section 15)

• To Lay on the Table or to Take from the Table (Section 19)

• The Previous Question (Section 20)

• To Reconsider (Section 27) a question that is itself undebatable

• Questions relating to Reading Papers (Section 16), Withdrawal of a Motion (Section 17), suspending the rules (see Section 18), extending the limits of debate (see Section 34), limiting or closing debate (see Section 37), or granting permission to continue a speech to someone guilty of indecorum in debate (see Section 36)

The motion to Postpone to a Certain Time (Section 21) allows only very limited debate that must focus on whether the postponement is appropriate. When an amendment is before an assembly, the main question can't be debated unless it's necessarily involved in the amendment. But the following motions will open to discussion the entire merits of the main question:

• To Commit (Section 22)

• To Postpone Indefinitely (Section 24)

• To Rescind (Section 25)

• To Reconsider a debatable question (Section 27)

It's important to keep in mind the distinction between debate and merely making suggestions or asking something. When asking something will help the assembly determine a question, it's allowed, to a limited extent, even though the question before the group is undebatable. Although free debate is allowed on every principal question (see Section 6), it's either permitted or prohibited on other questions according to these principles:

> English common parliamentary law makes all motions debatable unless some rule is adopted that limits debate. But every assembly is obliged to restrict debate on certain motions. The restrictions prescribed in Section 35 conform to the practice of Congress. There, however, it's very common to allow brief remarks on even the most undebatable questions, sometimes with five or six members speaking. This is permitted, though, only when no one objects.

- Usually, highly privileged questions shouldn't be debated. This is the case because they could be used to stop the assembly from voting on the main question. For example, if a motion to Adjourn (Section 11) were debatable, it could be used to hinder business. High privilege is generally not compatible with the right of debate on a privileged question.

- A motion that would suppress a question before the assembly so that it couldn't be taken up during the current session (see Section 42) should have and does allow for free debate. A subsidiary motion (see Section 7) except to Commit (see example below) is debatable just to the extent that it interferes with the right of the assembly to take up the original question when desired.

The following examples point out the effect of various motions and hence the need for (or need to avoid) debate:

Example: To Postpone [a matter] Indefinitely (Section 24) prevents an assembly from taking it up again during that session. Therefore, free debate should be and is allowed for this motion, even involving the whole merits of the original question.

Example: To Postpone [a matter] to a Certain Time (Section 21) prevents an assembly from considering a question until the designated time. Therefore, this motion should have and does allow for limited debate on the appropriateness of the postponement.

Example: To Lay [a matter] on the Table (Section 19) means that the assembly can consider it at any time. Therefore, this motion need not be and isn't debatable. (See Section 19 concerning abuse of this motion.)

Example: To Commit (Section 22) wouldn't be very debatable, according to the rule about opening the main question to debate. But it's an exception because it's often important for a committee to know the views of the assembly on a question. Thus it should be and not only is debatable, but it also opens to debate the whole question to be referred to the committee.

Section 36. Decorum in Debate

In debate you should confine yourself to the question before the assembly and avoid personalities. You shouldn't reflect on any act of the assembly unless you intend to make a motion to Rescind (Section 25) while debating or at the conclusion of your remarks.

When you refer to another member, avoid using the person's name; instead, refer to the member as "the member who spoke last" or by some other impersonal designation. Always refer to the officers of the assembly by their official titles (see Section 2).

Although you shouldn't question the motives of a member, you may strongly condemn the nature or consequences of some measure proposed by that member. In other words, it's not the person but the measure that's the subject of debate.

When the chair rises to state a point of order, give information, or say something else, within the limits of the chair's authority (see Section 40), the person speaking must sit down until the chair is heard first. When someone is called to order, that person must sit down until the question of order is decided. If the member's remarks are decided to be improper, that person may not continue speaking if anyone objects unless he or she gets the permission of the assembly (by majority vote); no debate is allowed on that question.

Disorderly words should be written down by the person who objects to them or by the clerk of the assembly and then read to the member. If the member denies having said them, the assembly will have to decide (by majority vote) whether or not they really are the member's words. If a member can't justify the words he or she used but won't apologize for using them, the assembly must take action. If the disorderly words are personal, involving another member, the two persons should leave the room. (It's a general rule that a person should not be present when an assembly is debating something about that person.) Then the assembly can proceed to deliberate the case. The person who objected to the words, however, doesn't have to leave unless he or she is one of the parties involved in the case. But if any business has taken place since the member spoke, it's too late to act on the disorderly words.

During debate and while the chair is speaking or the assembly is engaged in voting, no one is allowed to disturb the assembly by whispering or walking around or doing anything else that might be distracting or disruptive.

Section 37. Closing Debate

Debate on a question is *not* closed by the chair rising to put the question to a vote. Until *both* the affirmative and negative are "put," a member can claim the floor and reopen debate (see Section 38). Debate can be closed by the motions listed below. The first two close debate only by suppressing the question itself. (For the circumstances under which each of the motions should be used to suppress debate or suppress the questions, see Sections 58 and 59.) The motions given below can't be debated and, except for the motion to lay on the Table (Section 19), require a two-thirds vote to be adopted.

- An Objection to the Consideration of a Question (Section 15) is allowed only when the motion is first made. If the objection is sustained, it not only stops the debate but also throws the subject out of the assembly for the current session (see Section 42). This is the effect for which it was designed.

- To Lay [a matter] on the Table (Section 19), if adopted, carries the question to the table. For it to be taken from the table, there must be a majority vote.

- A call for the Previous Question (Section 20), if adopted, cuts off debate and brings the assembly to a vote on the matter being discussed. An exception would be when the pending motion is a motion to Amend (Section 23) or to Commit (Section 22). In that case, the vote is taken not only on the motion to Amend or Commit but also on the question to be amended or committed—unless someone demands that a vote be taken only on the motion to Amend or to Commit. When the Previous Question is ordered only on an amendment, or an amendment of an amendment (see Section 23), debate is closed and a vote is taken immediately on the amendment. The effect of the Previous Question is then exhausted (no longer exists), and new amendments can be offered and debated.

- An assembly can adopt an order to *limit debate* on a special subject in regard to the number or length of speeches. It can also decide to *close debate* on the subject at a stated time, and all pending questions must be put to a vote then without further debate. Either measure may be applied simply to a pending amendment or to an amendment of an amendment. When this is voted on, the original question is still open to debate and amendment.

In the House, where each member may speak for an hour, any of the motions to cut off debate can be adopted by a mere majority. In practice, however, they are not used until after some debate. Rule 28 of the House provides that forty minutes, twenty on each side, are allowed for debate whenever the Previous Question (Section 20) is ordered on a proposition for which there has been no debate or when the rules are suspended (see Section 18). In ordinary societies, harmony is so essential that a two-thirds vote should be required to force the assembly to a final vote without allowing free debate (see Section 39).

Article VI. Vote

Section 38. Voting

When it's not allowed to modify or debate a question, the chair should immediately put the motion to a vote. With a debatable question, however, the chair should wait until it appears that the debate has ended and then ask if the assembly is ready for the question. If no one rises or speaks, the chair can put the question to a vote.

Different parts of the country use different forms for "putting the question." The U.S. House of Representatives uses this form:

As many as are in favor [*as the question may be*] say aye.

After the ayes are said, the next question is:

As many as are opposed say no.

This form is very common in ordinary societies:

> **It has been moved and seconded that _____. Those in favor of the motion say aye. [*Pause for the yes vote*]. Those opposed say no.**

Suppose that a motion has been made to adopt a certain resolution. After it has been read, the chair will state:

> **You've heard the resolution read. Those in favor of its adoption raise their right hands. [*Pause for the yes vote*.] Those opposed do the same.**

These examples show the usual methods of putting a question, with the affirmative vote taken first. (See Section 65; see also Forms of Putting Certain Questions in the Quick-Reference Guide to Motions.)

A majority of the votes actually cast is sufficient to adopt any motion that's in order except those mentioned in Section 39; they require a two-thirds vote. A plurality vote never adopts a motion or elects anyone to office unless a special rule allowing it was adopted previously (see Section 39).

When a vote is taken, the chair should announce the results in a form similar to the following examples:

> **The motion is carried—the resolution is adopted.**

> **The ayes have it—the resolution is adopted.**

When the chair announces a vote, if anyone then rises and states that he or she doubts the vote or calls for a "division" of the question, the chair should put it to a vote:

> **A division is called for; those in favor of the motion will rise.**

After counting them and announcing the number, the chair would continue:

> **Those opposed will rise.**

The chair would next count the no votes, announce the number, and state whether the motion is carried or lost. The chair could also direct the secretary or appoint tellers to make the count and report the numbers to him or her. When tellers are appointed, they should be selected from both sides of a question—for and against. When a vote is not taken by ballot, members may change their votes but only *before* the decision of the question has been finally and conclusively pronounced by the chair.

Until the negative vote is taken, any member may rise and speak, make motions for amendment or otherwise, and thus renew the debate just as if voting had never started. This is true whether or not the member was in the room when the question was put and the affirmative vote taken. When a member rises to speak before the no votes are requested, therefore, the question is considered to be in the same state as if it had never been put.

Members can't vote on a question that affects them personally. But if more than one name is included in a resolution, all are entitled to vote. (A sense of etiquette would stop most people from exercising this right unless their vote was necessary to change the outcome.) Otherwise, a minority could control an assembly simply by including the names of a sufficient number of persons in a motion. This might occur, for example, with motions bringing charges against certain persons or even suspending or expelling them from the assembly. (After charges are preferred against a member and the assembly has ordered the person to appear for trial, the member is theoretically "in arrest," or restrained, and is deprived of all rights of membership until his or her case is disposed of.)

A motion fails if there's a tie vote unless the presiding officer, exercising the right of the chair to cast a deciding vote, votes yes. If the vote would cause a tie, however, the chair might cast a negative vote to defeat a measure.

When an Appeal (Section 14) is made concerning a decision the chair makes, he or she should ask:

Shall the decision of the chair stand as the judgment of the assembly?

In that case, a tie vote would uphold the chair's decision. The guiding principle is that a group can reverse a chair's decision only by majority vote; therefore, a tie vote (no majority) wouldn't be sufficient to reverse it, and that in effect would mean that the chair's decision would stand.

An assembly can also vote by ballot. This method of voting is used when a group's constitution or bylaws requires it or when an assembly has ordered that a vote be taken by ballot. To vote by ballot, the chair would appoint at least two tellers. They would distribute slips of paper on which the members, including the chair, would write their vote. If the chair should forget to vote when everyone else does, before the ballots are counted, he or she must get the permission of the assembly to vote afterwards. In voting for candidates in ordinary assemblies, the ballots may have incorrectly written names; nevertheless, they should be counted as a vote for the intended candidate whenever that intention is clear. In voting by ballot, members also may vote for persons who weren't nominated. Although closing nominations means that other candidates can't be endorsed publicly, it doesn't stop members from voting for others and electing them.

After the votes are collected, they're counted by the tellers. In counting the ballots, all blanks are ignored. The result is then reported to the chair, who announces it to the assembly. In the case of an election to office, the chair might state:

> **The whole number of votes cast is ____; the number necessary for election is ____. Mr. Castell received ____; Ms. Williams, ____; Mrs. Reuben, ____. Mr. Castell, having received the required number, is elected ____.**

When there's only one candidate for office and the organization's constitution requires a vote by ballot, it's common to authorize the clerk to cast the vote of the assembly for the one candidate. (If anyone objects, though, ballots must be handled in the usual way.) This can be done only by unanimous consent, and it's doubtful that it should even be allowed. When a motion is made to make a vote unanimous, therefore, it fails if anyone objects. An election, like other matters voted on, takes effect immediately unless there's a rule to the contrary.

By majority vote, an assembly can order that the vote on any question be taken by "yeas and nays." Voting by yeas and nays, a method peculiar to the United States, has the effect of placing on the record how each member votes. But it takes a great deal of time and is rarely useful in ordinary societies.

Under the U.S. Constitution, in both the House and the Senate one-fifth of the members present can order a vote to be taken by yeas and nays. To avoid some of the resulting inconveniences, Congress has required, for instance, that the Previous Question must be seconded by a majority. That step avoids taking the yeas and nays until a majority are in favor of ordering the main question. This method of voting is very useful in representative bodies, especially when the proceedings are published. It lets the people know how their representatives voted on important measures. If there's not a legal or constitutional provision in a representative body for a minority ordering the yeas and nays, the organization should adopt a rule allowing the yeas and nays to be ordered by one-fifth vote, as in Congress, or even a much smaller number. In some small bodies, a single member can demand that a vote on the resolution be taken by the yeas and nays.

To vote by yeas and nays, the chair must state both sides of the question at once. The clerk then calls the roll, and as each member's name is called, that person rises and answers yes (or aye) or no. After the roll call, the clerk would read the names of those who voted yes, followed by those who voted no. Any mistakes in the record are corrected before the clerk gives the number voting on each side to the chair, who will announce the result. With a vote by yeas and nays, an entry must be made in the minutes of all persons voting yes and all voting no.

The chair uses a form similar to this in putting a question to a vote by yeas and nays:

As many as are [*or* "Those"] in favor of the adoption of these resolutions will, when their names are called, answer yes [*or* "aye"]; those opposed will answer no.

The chair then directs the clerk to call the roll. Since both the affirmative and negative are "put" at the same time, as shown in the above example, it's too late for anyone to renew debate after one person has answered the roll call. Also, once the roll call begins, it's too late for anyone to ask to be excused from voting.

Voting by yeas and nays can never be used to hinder business as long as the above rule is observed. Moreover, it shouldn't be used at all in a mass meeting or in any other assembly where the members are not responsible to a constituency. The yeas and nays can't be ordered in a committee of the whole (see Section 32).

Section 39. Motions Requiring More Than a Majority Vote

A *majority* vote means a majority of the votes actually cast, just as a two-thirds vote refers to two-thirds of the votes actually cast. Blanks are never counted. Sometimes the bylaws of an organization provide for a vote of two-thirds of the members present or two-thirds of the members in the organization, both of which are very different requirements from one specifying two-thirds of the votes cast.

Example: Suppose that twelve members vote on a question in a meeting where twenty are present and the total membership is thirty. A two-thirds vote would be eight; a two-thirds vote of those present would be fourteen; a two-thirds

vote of the membership would be twenty. In this
case, a majority vote would be seven.

A *plurality* vote occurs when someone has more votes
for a certain office or position than any of the rivals. In
civil government, as a rule all officers elected by a popular vote are elected by a plurality. But in a deliberative
assembly, where voting may be repeated until someone is
elected, a plurality never elects unless there's a special
rule allowing it.

The following motions require a two-thirds vote to
be adopted since a mere majority shouldn't be able
to deprive others of the right to discuss something
and the right to have the rules enforced. Motions
other than those listed below, however, require only a
majority:

- To Amend the Rules (Section 45; also requires previous notice)

- To Suspend the Rules (Section 18)

- To make a Special Order (Sections 13, 61)

- To Take Up a Question Out of Its Proper Order
  (Section 13)

- An Objection to Consideration of a Question (Section 15; a negative vote on considering a question
  must be two-thirds to discuss the question for the
  current session)

- To Extend the Limits of Debate (Section 34)

- To Limit or Close Debate (Section 37)

- To call for the Previous Question (Section 20)

Every motion in the above list can suspend or change
some rule or custom of deliberative bodies. The first two,
by their title, obviously have the effect of changing a rule
or custom. But the others have a similar effect, even
though their title may not immediately suggest this.

Example: To make a Special Order suspends all of the rules that interfere with the consideration of a question at the specified time.

Example: To Take Up a Question Out of Its Proper Order is a change in the order of business.

Example: An Objection to the Consideration of a Question, if the motion passes, suspends or conflicts with the right of a member to introduce a measure in the assembly. That right has certainly been established by a custom and seems to be essential to the very idea of a deliberative body. (Although Rule 41 of the House allows a majority vote to decide this question, it is so important that representatives do not take advantage of the rule.)

Example: To Extend the Limits of Debate is to suspend a rule or order of an assembly.

Example: The Previous Question and motions to Close or Limit Debate force an assembly to take final action on a question without allowing discussion. In other words, they suspend the fundamental principle of deliberative bodies that an assembly won't be forced to take final action on a question until everyone has had a chance to discuss its merits. (Although a majority can stop debate by laying a question on the table, the assembly can take it from the table at any time. A majority of members, however, can still use this means to get rid of a question at least until they're ready to consider it.)

In spite of the need for members to be able to discuss questions, there are times when it's useful to suspend the right to introduce and debate matters just as it might be advantageous to suspend the rules of an assembly or change the order of business. Nevertheless, if a bare majority could suspend or change rules and privileges, those rules and privileges wouldn't be of much value.

Experience has shown that a two-thirds vote should be required to adopt any motion that could suspend or change the rules or established order of business, and the rule requiring a two-thirds vote on the motions listed above is based on this general principle.

Old parliamentary practice required unanimous consent for a suspension of the rules. The House requires only a majority to call for the Previous Question, to Close or Limit Debate, and to sustain an Objection to Consideration of a Question (a rule no longer taken advantage of). Because of the huge amount of business to be transacted and the larger number of members in the House, each entitled to speak in debate for an hour, it's necessary for them to allow a majority to Limit or Close Debate. This is especially significant in Congress, since the minority party could practically stop legislation if it could also prevent debate from being cut off. Groups that have partisan members should, like Congress, allow a bare majority to call for the Previous Question and to Limit or Close Debate. (See Section 38 in regard to ordering the yeas and nays by a one-fifth vote in Congress; see also the discussion of congressional procedure in the Introduction.)

Article VII. The Officers and the Minutes

Section 40. Chairman or President

When no special title has been assigned, the presiding officer is usually called the chairman (in religious assemblies, the moderator). Frequently, the assembly's constitution prescribes a title such as president. (See Section

34; also read Sections 2, 24, 44, and 65 in connection with this section.)

The presiding officer's duties are as follows:

- To open the session at the required time by taking the chair and calling the members to order

- To announce business before the assembly in the order it must be acted on (see Section 44)

- To state and put to a vote (see Sections 38 and 65) all motions that are made regularly and those that arise during the meeting

- To announce the result of a vote on motions

- To restrain members engaged in debate within the rules of order (when the disorder is so great that business can't be transacted and the chair can't enforce order, to adjourn the assembly as a last resort)

- To enforce order and decorum (see Section 36) on all occasions among the members

- To decide all Questions of Order (subject to an Appeal [Section 14] to the assembly by any two members)

- To inform the assembly about a point of order or practice when necessary or when called on to do so

- To authenticate by his or her signature, when necessary, all of the acts, orders, and proceedings of the assembly

- To represent and stand for the assembly in general, declaring its will and always obeying its rules

Formally, the chair rises (stands up) to put a question to a vote but may remain seated. (In very small groups, though, such as a committee or board of trustees, the chair usually wouldn't stand up.) The presiding officer also rises (without calling anyone forward) when speaking on a Question of Order (the chair is entitled to speak before other members when he or she chooses to do so). The chair always refers to himself or herself as "the chair," not "I":

> **The chair has decided that ...** [*not* **"I have decided that ..."**]

When a member has the floor, the chair can't interrupt as long as the member doesn't break any rules of the assembly (except as described in Section 2).

The chair may vote when voting is done by ballot and in all other cases when the vote would change the result. (But the chair must vote *before* the tellers have started to count the ballots; otherwise, the permission of the assembly is needed.)

> *Example:* Suppose that a two-thirds vote is needed to pass a motion and the chair's vote with the minority would cause the motion to fail. In that case the chair is entitled to vote since doing so would change the result. In the same way, the chair may vote with the minority if doing so would create a tie vote. That would also cause the motion to fail, since it must have a majority or two-thirds vote depending on the specific motion and the applicable requirement.

If someone makes a motion that refers to the chair, the presiding officer shouldn't put the question to a vote. Instead, either the secretary must put the question, or if the secretary doesn't do it, the person making the motion may put it to a vote.

If the presiding officer has to leave, he or she may appoint a chairman pro tem. But the first adjournment puts an end to that appointment, and the assembly can end it earlier by electing another chair. When there are vice-presidents, however, the first one on the list who is present acts as chair in the absence of the regular presiding officer and should always be called to the chair in such cases.

The regular chair, knowing that he or she will be

absent from a future meeting, nevertheless may not authorize another member to fill in. In such a case—when there are no vice-presidents—the clerk (see Section 4) or, in the clerk's absence, any member at this future meeting should call the meeting to order and see to it that a chairman pro tem is elected. The chairman pro tem would then hold office during that session (see Section 42) unless or until the regular chairman returned. Again, the exception would be that if there were vice-presidents in the meeting, instead of a chairman pro tem being elected the first vice-president on the list would be called to assume the chair.

The presiding officer sometimes calls a member to take over the chair so that he or she can take part in the debate. As a rule, though, this shouldn't be done. Moreover, it never should be done when the members clearly object to it or when there might be difficulty in preserving order because of it. Whenever a chair gives the appearance of being partisan, he or she loses much of the ability to control the opposition. (See Section 28 for the duties of committee chairs.)

Many presiding officers have a bad habit of speaking on questions before the assembly, even interrupting a member who has the floor. This is unjustified in both common parliamentary law and the practice of Congress. Someone who expects to take an active part in debate shouldn't accept the position of chair.

It is a general rule in all deliberative assemblies that the presiding officer shall not participate in the debate, or other proceedings, in any other capacity than as such officer. He is only allowed, therefore, to state matters of fact within his knowledge; to inform the assembly on points of order or the course of proceeding, when called upon for that purpose, or when he finds it necessary to do so; and, on appeals from his decision on questions of order, to address the assembly in debate. (Cushing's Manual, Section 202)

Though the speaker [chair] may of right speak to matters of order and be first heard, he is restrained from speaking on any other subject except where the assembly have occasion for facts within his knowledge; then he may, with their leave, state the matter of fact. (Jefferson's Manual, Section xvii; and Barclay's "Digest of the Rules and Practice of the House of Representatives U.S.," page 195)

The chair should be familiar with parliamentary usage and set an example of conforming strictly to it. But no rules will take the place of tact and common sense. A chair usually wouldn't wait for routine motions or for a motion to be seconded when it's clearly favored by others (see Section 65). But if others object to proceeding in that manner, it's safer to insist instantly that the forms of parliamentary law be observed. Although many things can be done by general consent to save time, when an assembly is large or divided, and when some members are continually raising points of order, the best course is to enforce strictly all of the rules and forms of parliamentary law.

When an improper motion is made, the chair shouldn't simply rule it out of order. Instead, the chair should suggest the best way to accomplish whatever is intended:

Example: Suppose that someone moves to postpone the question. The chair should explain that if the time isn't specified, the proper motion is for the question to Lay on the Table (Section 19).

Example: Suppose that someone moves to Lay [a question] on the Table until a certain time. The chair should suggest that the proper motion is to Postpone [the question] to a Certain Time (Section 21).

Example: Suppose that someone moves to reject a resolution. The chair should state that the question is to Postpone [the resolution] Indefinitely (Section 24) since that's the parliamentary form of the question.

A chair also should have executive ability and be capable of controlling people. But to control others, one has to control one's self. An excited chair will likely cause trouble in a meeting. (For hints to inexperienced chairs, see Section 50.)

A chair shouldn't let the object of a meeting be defeated by people who are using parliamentary forms to obstruct business. In such a case, the chair should refuse to entertain a dilatory motion (one that causes delay). If an appeal is made by the opposition, though, the chair should entertain it. But if the chair's decision is sustained by a large majority, he or she can then refuse to entertain any further appeal made by the faction while it's continuing its obstruction. The chair shouldn't, however, adopt such a course merely to expedite business when the opposition isn't trying to obstruct the proceedings.

Sometimes a presiding officer is perplexed with the difficulties that go with the position of chair. In such cases it's best to heed the advice of a distinguished writer on parliamentary law who said:

> The great purpose of all rules and forms is to subserve the will of the assembly rather than to restrain it; to facilitate, and not to obstruct, the expression of their deliberate sense.

Section 41. Clerk, or Secretary, and the Minutes

The officer who records the proceedings of a meeting is usually called the clerk or secretary, and the record of the meeting is called the minutes. When there are two secretaries, the one who records the meeting activity is called the recording secretary. The other one is called the corresponding secretary. In many organizations the secretary not only acts as recording officer but also collects the dues of members. To that extent the secretary is also a financial officer. In most cases the treasurer acts as banker, paying bills only on the order of the organization, signed by the secretary alone or by the president and secretary. In such cases the secretary becomes in reality the financial officer and should report to the organization on income received and its source as well as money spent and why. (See Section 52 for the secretary's duties as financial officer.)

The secretary's desk should be near that of the chair. If the chair is absent and there is no vice-president attending the meeting, the secretary should call the meeting to order when the time for opening the session arrives. The secretary would then preside until the assembly elects a chairman pro tem, which should be done immediately.

The secretary should keep a record of the proceedings (see Section 51), which might begin like this:

> **At a regular quarterly meeting of [*organization*], held on the 31st day of March 19XX, at [*place*], with [*name of president or chair*] presiding, the minutes were read by the clerk and approved.**

If the regular clerk had been absent, the wording might be as follows:

> **A regular quarterly meeting of [*organization*] was held on the 31st day of March 19XX, at [*place*], with [*name of president or chair*] presiding. The clerk being absent, [*name*] was appointed clerk pro tem. The minutes were then read and approved.**

If the minutes were not read, the statement about the minutes should be changed to something like this:

> **The reading of the minutes was dispensed with.**

The essential points to make in the opening paragraph of the minutes are the following:

- The kind of meeting: regular (quarterly, biannual, or the like) or special; or adjourned regular or adjourned special

- The name of the assembly

- The date and place of the meeting (place can be omitted if it is always the same)

- The fact of the presence of the regular chair and clerk or, in their absence, the name of their substitutes

- Whether or not the minutes of the previous meeting were read and approved

The person responsible for writing the minutes should write them neatly with ink, leaving a margin for corrections. (Depending on the organization and the type of meeting, notes may be taken in longhand, in shorthand, or by machine. Recordings, however, should always be backed up by notes.) The notes would be transferred to a permanent minute book, and the minutes would then be taken to the next meeting of the organization to be read for corrections and approval. In many organizations, though, the secretary keeps the original notes taken during the meeting in a pocket memo book that can be carried to every meeting. These original notes, as corrected, are approved and then transferred into a permanent record. This plan results in neater records, but the original notes should always be kept until they're compared carefully with the permanent record. After an assembly approves the minutes, without a reconsideration, the society may correct them further at any future time no matter how much time has elapsed or how many times they have already been amended. The official version of the minutes (not the original notes) must be signed by the person who acted as clerk for that meeting. In some organizations, the chair must also sign the minutes. When they're published, both officers should sign them.

In deciding how to keep the minutes, a lot depends on the kind of meeting and whether the minutes will be published. Regardless, the clerk must never use the minutes personally to commend or criticize something said or done in a meeting. If the minutes are going to be published it's often far more interesting to know what leading speakers said rather than what resolutions were adopted or what routine business was transacted. In such cases, the secretary may need at least one assistant to help prepare the minutes for publication. (For additional information on minutes and conference proceedings, see the fourth chapter in the first part of the book, "Meeting Arrangements: Practices and Procedures.")

In meetings of ordinary groups or boards of managers and trustees, however, there is no point in reporting debates. The clerk in such cases primarily records what is done, not what is said. Unless some rule states otherwise, the clerk should enter every principal motion (see Section 6) that comes before the assembly, whether it's adopted or rejected.

When there's a division (see Section 38) or when the vote is by ballot, the clerk should enter the number of votes on each side. When the voting is by "yeas and nays" (see Section 38), the clerk should enter a list of the names of those voting on each side.

The clerk should note on committee reports the date they were received, state what further action was taken on them, and preserve them among the various records that are the clerk's responsibility. Then, in the minutes, the clerk should summarize any report that was agreed to unless the report contains resolutions. In that case, the resolutions should be entered in full as adopted by the assembly but not as though it were the report that was accepted. With a particularly important report, however, the assembly should order it "to be entered in the minutes." The clerk would then include the full report. But the proceedings of a committee of the whole (see Section 32) or while acting informally (see Section 33) should *not* be entered in the minutes.

Before an adjournment "without day [*sine die*]," when it will be a long time until the next meeting, the clerk usually reads the current minutes for approval, rather than wait until the next meeting. But if the next meeting will be held within a reasonable time, the clerk should wait and read them at the next meeting. They would be adopted then (after being corrected, if necessary). If errors are discovered later, the minutes should be corrected again, no matter how much time has elapsed or how many times previously they were corrected. The corrections are handled, without making a motion to Reconsider, by a simple vote to amend the minutes.

The secretary has custody of the minutes and all other official documents that come before a deliberative assembly. Every member, however, has the right to inspect the minutes, and the chair can even order that certain minutes must be turned over to a committee that needs them to perform its duties.

Before each meeting the clerk should prepare an order of business (see Section 44) for the chair to use. This would show everything expected to come before the assembly, each item in its exact order. The clerk also should bring to each meeting a list of all standing committees and any existing select committees. When another committee is appointed, the clerk should hand to the committee chair or some other committee member(s) the names of the committee members and all papers referred to the committee.

Article VIII. Miscellaneous

Section 42. Session

A *session* of an assembly is a meeting, or a number of adjourned meetings, that may last several days (e.g., a session of a convention) or several months (e.g., a session of Congress) but altogether is considered *one* unit. The term *meeting* refers to an assembling together of members of a deliberative body for any length of time with no separation by adjournment. An ajournment to meet later, even the same day, ends the meeting but *not* the session, since the session includes all of the adjourned meetings. The *next* meeting, then, would be an "adjourned meeting" of the *same* session.

A meeting ends by temporary adjournment; a session, which may consist of many meetings, ends by adjournment "without day." A *recess* is a pause or break in the proceedings taken for perhaps a few minutes. But it doesn't end a meeting. The intermediate adjournments from day to day or the recesses taken during the day, therefore, don't destroy the continuity of a meeting—in reality, they make up one session. Any meeting that is *not* an adjournment of another meeting begins a new session. But in a permanent organization that has regular meetings every week, month, or year, for example, each individual meeting constitutes a separate session of the organization. That session, however, can be prolonged by adjourning to another day.

Under ordinary circumstances you can end a meeting simply by moving to Adjourn (Section 11). The group may meet again at the time specified by the organization's rules or by a resolution that sets the time. If the group doesn't meet until the time specified in the bylaws for the next regular meeting, an adjournment is said to close the session and, in effect, is an adjournment "without day." But if the group had previously set a time for the next meeting by vote or by adopting a program that covers several meetings (or days), the adjournment is, in effect, "to a certain day." It, therefore, does *not* close the session. When an assembly has meetings several days in a row, they all constitute one session.

If a principal motion (see Section 6) is postponed indefinitely (see Section 24) or rejected in one session, it can't be introduced again at that particular session (see Section 26). But it can be introduced at the next session as long as a rule of the assembly doesn't prohibit it. So a question that was laid on the table (see Section 19) at one session can be introduced as a new motion at any succeeding session. The only way to introduce that question at the same session would be to move to Take it from the Table (see Section 19).

No session may interfere with the assembly's rights at any future session unless the constitution, bylaws, or rules of order allow it. Such documents aren't changed suddenly—they require notice of any proposed amendment and then at least a two-thirds vote for adoption—rather, they're considered an expression of the deliberative views of an entire organization, not merely the opinions or wishes of any particular meeting. So if a presiding officer were temporarily ill, for instance, an assembly couldn't elect another chair to hold office for longer than the current session. By following the prescribed steps for an *election* to fill a vacancy, however, giving whatever notice is necessary, an assembly could legally elect a chair to hold office as long as the regular chair was absent.

Although one session of an assembly can't control or dictate to the next session of the assembly, any session may adopt a permanent rule or resolution that continues in force until it's rescinded (see Section 49). Nevertheless, these standing rules won't interfere with future sessions since a majority can suspend or rescind them (see Section 25) or adopt new standing rules at any moment. So there's no justification for an assembly postponing anything to a day beyond the next succeeding session in an attempt to stop the next session from considering a question. On the other hand, one may not move to Reconsider (Section 27) a vote taken at a previous session. But the motion to Reconsider can be called up if it was made at the last meeting of the previous session. Also, committees may be appointed to report at a future session.

In all legislative bodies, including Congress, the limits of a session are clearly defined. In permanent ordinary societies, however, with more or less frequent meetings, this matter causes a lot of confusion. Any organization may decide what constitutes a session. But if there's no rule clarifying this, common parliamentary law would make each regular or special meeting a *separate* session.

There are significant disadvantages to a rule that makes a session include all of the meetings of an ordinary society over a long period such as a year (see Sections 24 and 26). The members of an organization might take advantage of the freedom that comes from considering each regular meeting a separate session but then might repeatedly renew unprofitable motions. In that case, the group could adopt a rule prohibiting the second introduction of any principal question (see Section 6) within, say, three or six months after its rejection or after indefinite postponement or after the society refused to consider it. Generally, though, it's better to suppress the undesirable question simply by making another motion refusing to consider it (see Section 15).

Section 43. Quorum

A *quorum* in an assembly is the number needed to transact business. Unless there's a special rule to the contrary, the quorum of every assembly is a majority of all members. A permanent society, however, usually adopts a smaller number as a quorum, often less than one-twentieth of the members. A small number for a quorum is necessary in large groups because only a small percentage of the members are ever present at a meeting. Although a quorum may transact any business, it's usually best not to transact important business unless the meeting has a fair attendance (more than a quorum) or unless previous notice of the proposed action was given. To act by unanimous consent, at least a quorum has to be present.

In the English Parliament, the House of Lords (about four hundred and fifty members) can transact business if only three members are present. The House of Commons (about six hundred and seventy members) requires only forty members for a quorum. But the U.S. Constitution (Article 1, Section 5) states that a majority of each house of Congress is needed for a quorum to do business.

The presiding officer at a meeting shouldn't take the chair until a quorum is present unless there's no hope of a quorum attending. Then no business can be transacted except to Adjourn (Section 11). If no one objects, debate may continue, but the only vote that may be taken is the one for adjournment.

In a committee of the whole, the quorum requirement is the same as for the assembly. In any other committee, a majority is required unless the assembly orders otherwise. Also, a committee has to wait for a quorum before proceeding to undertake its business. If later in a meeting the number falls below quorum requirements, business isn't interrupted unless a member points it out. Nevertheless, no question can be decided (voted on) unless a quorum is present.

Boards of trustees, managers, directors, and the like usually have the same quorum requirement as a committee—a majority of the members. The organization that appoints a board delegates its power to it and decides what number is needed for it to transact business. Therefore, the organization could decide on a number other than a majority. But if it doesn't specify another number, the requirement is considered to be a majority.

It's important to be careful in amending the rule about a quorum. An assembly might want to change the quorum requirement from one number to another. If it acts first to strike out the old number, not specifying the new number at the same time, the quorum requirement instantly becomes a majority. The problem is that it may not ever be possible to get a majority together to make the desired change. Without a majority, then, there won't be a quorum to transact business and adopt the new rule specifying a different number for a quorum. The proper procedure, instead, to amend a rule about the quorum is to strike out certain words (or the whole rule) and insert certain other words (or the new rule)—all at the same time. In that way the matter will be voted on as one question.

Section 44. Order of Business

Every permanent society must adopt an order of business (the order in which things will be considered) for its meetings. When an organization doesn't do this, the following order should be followed:

- Reading of the minutes (if several meetings a day are held, it's sufficient to read the minutes just once, usually at the first meeting of the day)

- Reports of standing committees (boards of managers, trustees, and so on are in this category)

- Reports of select committees

- Unfinished business (Orders of the Day [Section 13], which includes business postponed to the current meeting, is in this category)

- New business

If a subject has been made a Special Order (Section 13) for the day, it has precedence over all other business except the reading of the minutes.

If you want to transact business out of the specified order, it's necessary to move to Suspend the Rules (Section 18); that requires a two-thirds vote. But as each resolution or report comes up, a majority can immediately lay it on the table (see Section 19). They can thereby keep moving things out of the way until reaching the question they want to consider first. It's improper, though, to lay on the table or postpone an entire class of questions (such as committee reports). In fact, it's improper to put aside anything except the question currently before the assembly (see Section 19).

Section 45. Amendments of Rules of Order

Rules of order may be amended at any regular meeting of an assembly by two-thirds vote provided that the amendment was submitted *in writing* at the previous regular meeting. At least equal notice and a two-thirds vote are needed to amend a constitution or bylaws of an organization.

A constitution, bylaws, or set of rules of order should contain a provision that they can't be amended by less than a two-thirds vote and without previous notice of the proposed amendment. The notice is meant to let the members know what the amendment is and that it's going to be considered and acted on at a certain time.

Notice isn't required to amend the original amendment. If that were the case, it would be virtually impossible to amend the constitution, bylaws, or set of rules. Also, the amendment to the original amendment has to be relevant to that original amendment. No other amendment is in order or may delay action on the original amendment.

Often an organization's bylaws state that an amendment has to be read at a certain number of regular meetings before it can be acted on; the first reading is by the clerk when it's proposed. After the last reading it's up for action. If an amendment has to be read at three regular meetings, for instance, in a society that holds regular weekly meetings, action on it would be delayed until two weeks after it was first proposed.

Part II. Organization and Conduct of Business

Article IX. Organization and Meetings

Section 46. Occasional or Mass Meeting

Organization. Not all meetings are held by members of an organized society. When no organized society is involved, and various persons simply meet to conduct business, someone (anyone) in the group should start the meeting by stepping forward and stating:

> **The meeting will please come to order. I move that [*name of someone present*] act as chair of this meeting.**

Someone else should reply:

> **I second the motion.**

The person making the motion then puts the question to a vote:

> **It has been moved and seconded that [*name*] act as chair of this meeting. Those in favor say aye. [*Pause for the affirmative vote.*] Those opposed say no.**

If the majority votes in favor, the person who started the meeting states:

The motion is carried. [*Name*] will take the chair.

If the motion fails, he or she will announce that fact and ask that someone else be nominated. The above process is then repeated. (The dialogue in this section is a suggested wording for people in ordinary meetings. Although it's a common and proper form, the exact wording may vary.)

Sometimes a member of a group nominates a chair and no vote is taken. The assembly simply signifies approval by acclamation—applause, cheers, and the like. Also, the person who starts the meeting doesn't have to nominate someone. The temporary chair might instead state:

The meeting will please come to order. Will someone nominate a chair?

After receiving a nomination, it should be put to a vote as described above. In a large assembly, the person who does the nominating and one other member often escort the new presiding officer to the chair. The presiding officer then makes a short speech thanking the assembly for the honor.

Assume that Mr. Ver Meer was elected chair in an ordinary meeting. The first thing he should do is see to it that a secretary is elected. He or someone else would then make a motion nominating someone for this post. After that, several names may be called out, and Mr. Ver Meer would name each person nominated: "Mrs. Blumenthal is nominated; Ms. Wright is nominated; Mr. Pendleton is nominated;" and so on. After naming each nominee, he would "put the question" as follows, taking a vote on each one in the order nominated:

Those in favor of Mrs. Blumenthal acting as secretary of this meeting will say aye. [*Pause for the affirmative vote.*] Those opposed say no.

If the motion is lost, the question is "put" on Ms. Wright and so on until someone is elected. Following election, the secretary should take a seat near the chair and keep a record of the proceedings (as described in Section 51).

Adoption of Resolutions. Usually, a chair and a secretary are the only two officers needed for an ordinary meeting, so when the secretary is elected, the chair should immediately focus on the purpose of the meeting, as shown in these examples:

> **What business is there to consider?**
>
> **Will Ms. Anderson please explain the object of this meeting?**

At this point, if the meeting is merely a public assembly called together to consider some special subject, someone would offer a series of previously prepared resolutions or else move to appoint a committee to prepare them. In the first case, the exchange would resemble this:

> *Mr. Brent (addressing the chair):* **Mr. Chairman.**
>
> *Chair (recognizing the member):* **Mr. Brent.**

The member now has the floor and can make his motion:

> *Mr. Brent:* **I move that we adopt the following resolutions** [*he reads them and hands them to the chair*].
>
> *Ms. Schott:* **I second the motion.**

The chair sometimes directs the secretary to read the resolutions again and then states:

> **The question is on the adoption of the resolutions just read.** [*No one rises or speaks immediately so he adds this:*] **Are you ready for the question?** [*Again, no one rises or speaks so he puts the question to a vote.*] **Those in favor of the adoption of the resolutions just read will say**

aye. [*Pause for the yes vote.*] Those opposed will say no.

The chair then announces the result of the vote as in these examples:

The motion is carried—the resolutions are adopted.

The ayes have it—the resolutions are adopted.

In legislative bodies all resolutions, bills, and so on are sent to the clerk's desk. The title of the bill and the name of the member introducing it would be written on each one. In such bodies, however, there are several clerks and only one chair. In many assemblies there is only one clerk or secretary. Since that one person also has to keep the minutes, it's a mistake to keep interrupting the clerk to read every resolution offered. In such assemblies, unless some rule or established custom requires otherwise, it's permissible and much better to hand all resolutions, reports, and so on directly to the chair. If they were read by the member introducing them and no one had asked for another reading, the chair could omit reading them, assuming it's clear that they're fully understood. (For the manner of reading and stating a question when a resolution has several paragraphs, see Section 44.)

Committee to Draft Resolutions. Sometimes resolutions haven't been prepared, and it's best to have a committee draft them. In that case, someone should address the chair and, after being recognized, move to appoint a committee:

I move that a committee be appointed to draft resolutions reflecting the views of this meeting on [*subject*].

After the motion is seconded the chair states the question (see Section 65) and asks:

Are you ready for the question [*or* "Is there any discussion"]?

If no one rises or speaks the chair puts the question to a vote and announces the result. Assuming that it carried and that the motion didn't specify any number of members for the committee, the chair should next ask:

How many shall be on the committee?

If only one number is suggested, the chair simply announces that the committee will consist of that number. If several numbers are suggested, though, the chair should state each one and take a vote on each number, starting with the largest number and continuing until one of them is approved. The chair would then inquire:

How shall the committee be appointed?

The matter of appointment is usually decided informally (no vote). The committee might be appointed by the chair, in which case the chair would simply name the committee without any vote. Or the committee might be nominated by the chair or a member of the assembly. (A member may not name more than one person, except by unanimous consent.) The assembly would then vote on their appointment.

When the chair does the nominating, he or she states the names and puts the question to a vote concerning the entire committee:

Those in favor of these people constituting the committee say aye. [*Pause for the yes vote.*] Those opposed say no.

When nominations are made by members of the assembly, more names may be mentioned than the number selected for the committee. In that case a separate vote must be taken on each name, in the order nominated. (In a mass meeting, it's safer to have all committees appointed by the chair.)

Once a committee is appointed, the members should leave immediately, go to work, and agree on a report. This report should be written out as described in Section

53. During their absence, though, the assembly may take care of other business or spend the time listening to speeches. If the chair notices the committee returning to the room, he or she should wait for anyone who is speaking to stop and then announce that the assembly is ready to hear the committee's report or resolutions. Or the chair might first ask the committee if it's ready to report.

The committee chair should take the first opportunity to obtain the floor (see Section 2). This person is the one named first to be on the committee and often is the one who earlier moved to appoint the committee. After the assembly's presiding officer recognizes the committee chair, he or she would state:

The committee appointed to draft resolutions is ready to report.

The presiding officer then would state that the assembly "will now hear the report." The committee chair would read the report and hand it to the presiding officer. At that moment the committee is automatically dissolved without any action by the assembly.

Someone in the assembly should next move to adopt or accept the report or to agree to the resolution. Any such motion has the same effect. If it carries, the resolutions prepared by the committee become the resolutions of the assembly just as if the committee had nothing to do with them. (See Section 30 for common errors in acting on reports.) After the member makes the motion the presiding officer states the question and puts it to a vote as described earlier. It isn't necessary to adopt the resolutions immediately, however. The assembly, in fact, may want to debate them, modify them, postpone consideration of them, or do something else (see Sections 55–63).

When all business that the assembly met to handle is finished or when there's another reason to close the meeting, someone should move to Adjourn (Section 11). If the motion carries and no other time for meeting again is set, the chair would state:

The motion is carried. This assembly stands adjourned without day.

Another method for conducting a meeting is shown in Section 48.

Additional Officers. Perhaps more officers are needed than only a chair and secretary. They can be appointed in the manner described for the chair and secretary. Or the assembly can first form a temporary organization by electing a chairman pro tem and a secretary pro tem. As soon as a secretary pro tem is elected, then, a committee should be appointed to nominate the permanent officers (e.g., in a convention; see Section 47). The presiding officer is usually called the president, and sometimes numerous vice-presidents are appointed merely for complimentary purposes. In large, formal meetings, these vice-presidents sit on the platform next to the president. When the president is away or gives up the chair, the first person on the list of vice-presidents who is present should take the chair. (Readers who are pressed for time could, for now, skip Sections 47 through 53 and continue reading at Section 54.)

Section 47. Meeting of a Convention or Assembly of Delegates

Sometimes members of an assembly are elected or appointed to attend a meeting. It's necessary then to find out who is actually a member and is entitled to vote before the permanent organization is formed. First, a temporary organization is formed by electing a chairman pro tem and a secretary pro tem. The chairman pro tem then announces:

The next order of business is the appointment of a committee on credentials.

Someone next makes a motion to that effect:

> I move that a committee of three on the credentials of members be appointed by the chair and that the committee report as soon as possible.

Or the motion might be less detailed:

> I move that a committee of three be appointed on the credentials of members.

Either way, the chairman pro tem proceeds as described in the material about committees to draft resolutions (see Section 46).

When the time comes to vote on a motion to accept the committee's report, the only persons who may vote are those that the committee reports as having proper credentials. The committee may do more than list the members with proper credentials (fulfilling the voting requirements). It may also report doubtful or contested cases, with recommendations about them that the assembly may adopt, reject, postpone, or handle otherwise. But only the members who have an undisputed right to their seats may vote.

After the assembly disposes of the credentials question, at least temporarily, the chairman pro tem states:

> The next order of business is the election of permanent officers of the assembly.

Someone then moves to appoint a committee to nominate the officers; for example:

> I move that a committee of three be appointed by the chairman pro tem to nominate permanent officers of this convention.

If the motion carries, the appointed committee will meet to prepare a report. As soon as the committee makes its report, someone should move for its acceptance:

> I move that the report of the committee be accepted and that the officers nominated be declared the officers of the convention.

When members are competing for the offices, however, it's better to elect the officers by ballot. In this case, after the nominating committee reports, someone could make a motion as in the following examples (see Section 38 for balloting and other methods of voting):

> I move that the convention now proceed to the balloting for its permanent officers.

> I move that we now proceed to the election, by ballot, of the permanent officers of this convention.

The constitutions of permanent societies usually require that the officers be elected by ballot. If the motion to proceed to the election carries, the chairman pro tem immediately calls the new presiding officer to the chair. The temporary secretary is replaced at the same time, and the convention is then ready for its work.

Section 48. A Permanent Society

First Meeting. When one or more persons want to form a permanent society, they should see to it that only the appropriate interested persons are invited to be present at a certain time and place. Usually, in mass meetings or meetings called to organize a society, one waits ten to fifteen minutes after the appointed time. Then someone steps forward and states:

> The meeting will please come to order. I move that [*name*] act as chair of the meeting.

Someone seconds the motion, and the person who made the motion puts the question to a vote (see Section 46). If, for example, Ms. Channing is elected as chair, she announces that the election of a secretary is the first order of business.

After the secretary is elected, the chair calls on the person most interested in forming the society to state the object of the meeting or that person may make the first move:

> **Mr. Jacobs (addressing the chair): Madam Chairman.**
>
> **Chair (recognizing the member): Mr. Jacobs.**
>
> **Mr. Jacobs: We're meeting here today to discuss the formation of a new society . . .**

The chair might also ask others to give their opinions, and sometimes the members themselves call for a certain person to comment. The chair should note the wishes of the assembly but, without being too strict, should also be certain that someone doesn't speak so long that the other members become tired and impatient.

When enough time has been spent, informally, in listening to comments, someone should offer a resolution so that definite action can be taken. Those persons who want to get the meeting going, especially if it's going to be a large meeting, should have previously agreed on what they want done. They should be ready, at the proper time, to offer a suitable resolution:

> **RESOLVED, That it is the expressed opinion of this meeting that a society for [*purpose*] should now be formed in this city.**

This resolution would then be seconded and stated by the chair. It then is open to debate and should be voted on as described earlier (see Section 46). If the meeting is very large, it might be better to offer the resolution at the start of the meeting and skip the informal discussion.

After voting on the above motion, or even before that motion is offered, someone may propose the following:

> **I move that a committee of five be appointed by the chair to draft a constitution and bylaws for a society for [*purpose*] and that they report at an adjourned meeting of this assembly.**

This motion may be amended (see Section 56) by striking out and adding words and so on. It's also debatable.

When the committee to draft a constitution and bylaws is appointed, the chair may ask something such as this:

Is there any other business to discuss?

When all business is finished, someone should move to Adjourn (Section 11) to meet at a certain place and time. This motion, however, after being seconded and stated by the chair, is open to debate and amendment. A better alternative, therefore, might be to fix the time of the next meeting earlier in the proceedings. Then, when business is finished, someone can move simply to Adjourn, which by itself can't be amended or debated. If the motion to Adjourn carries, the chair should state:

This meeting stands adjourned to meet at [*time and place*].

Second Meeting. Ordinary meetings of an organized society are conducted like the second meeting (the chair, however, always announces business in the order specified in the society's rules [see Section 44]). At the second meeting, the officers of the previous meeting still serve (if present) until new permanent officers are elected. When it's time to start the meeting, the chair from the previous meeting stands and states:

The meeting will please come to order.

As soon as the people are seated and quiet, he or she adds:

The secretary will read the minutes of the last meeting.

If someone notices an error in the minutes, that person should point it out as soon as the secretary finishes reading. If no one objects, the chair can simply direct the secretary to make the correction without waiting for someone to make such a motion. After that, the chair would state:

> **If there's no objection, the minutes will stand approved as read [*or "corrected," if that's the case*].**

The chair would then announce the next item on the agenda, for example:

> **The next order of business is hearing reports from the standing committees.**

The chair may ask each committee, in their order, to make a report:

> **Does the Membership [*or other*] Committee have a report to make?**

The committee will either report or state that it has nothing to report. Since some or even all of the committees may have nothing to report, the chair could save time by asking generally:

> **Do any committees have reports to make?**

If no one rises to report, the chair could then move on:

> **Since there are no reports from the standing committees, the next item will be to hear reports of select committees.**

The same procedure can be followed in asking select committees for reports. At every meeting the chair should have a list of the committees to use in calling on them for reports and also as a guide in appointing new committees.

Perhaps some committee, such as the Constitution and Bylaws Committee, will want to report at the meeting. The committee chair would address the presiding officer of the assembly (Mr. or Madame Chairman) and, after being recognized, would read the report and then hand it to the presiding officer. If no one makes a motion, the presiding officer should ask what the assembly wants to do as shown in these examples:

> **You've heard the report read—what shall we do with it [*or* "what shall be done with it"]?**

> **You've heard the report read—what order shall be taken on it?**

In large, formal meetings, the chair would usually ask the secretary to read the report again before asking what to do with it. (See Section 30 for common errors in acting on reports; see also Section 46.) But in an ordinary assembly, someone presumably would move to adopt it at this time or, using the above example, would move "to adopt the constitution reported by the committee." After this motion is seconded, the presiding officer of the assembly should state the question:

> **The question is on the adoption of the constitution reported by the committee.**

He or she would then read the first article of the constitution and ask:

> **Are there any amendments proposed to this article?**

If none is offered, the chair would go on to the next article and so on until each one has been read and made available for amendment. (If articles are subdivided into sections or paragraphs, the amendments also should be made by sections or paragraphs.) The entire document would then be open for amendment:

> **The whole constitution, having been read, is open to amendment.**

Anyone is free at that time to move to amend any part of the constitution. When the chair believes everyone is finished, he or she should ask:

Are you ready for the question?

If no one wants to speak, the chair will assume that the assembly is ready and will put the question to a vote:

Those in favor of adopting the constitution as amended will say aye. [*Pause for yes vote.*] Those opposed will say no.

The chair should announce the result of the vote distinctly.

If the assembly voted to adopt the constitution as amended, the chair immediately should state that it has been adopted and those who want to become members must sign it (and pay any initiation fee required by the constitution). If the assembly is large, the chair may suggest a recess to give people time to sign. Someone could move to take a recess for ten (or other) minutes or until the constitution is signed. Once the document is signed, no one may vote at this meeting except those who signed it.

After the recess the chair must call the meeting to order again and state the next item to handle:

The next order of business is the adoption of the bylaws.

Someone should then move to adopt the bylaws reported by the committee, with the chair following the same steps as those for adopting a constitution. Afterwards, the chair should ask about further business, as shown in these examples:

Is there any further business to come before this meeting?

What is the further pleasure of the meeting?

Or the chair might simply state that the next item of business is the election of permanent officers of the society. Either way, if that's the next order of business, someone should move to appoint a committee to nominate the permanent officers of the society (see Section 47 for handling such a motion). As each officer is elected he or she replaces the temporary officer. When they're all elected, the organization of the new society is considered to be completed.

If a society intends to own real estate, it should be incorporated according to the laws of the state in which it's located. In fact, someone on the Constitution and Bylaws Committee should consult an attorney before the second meeting is held to be sure the constitution conforms to the law. In this case, the trustees are usually instructed to take the proper measures to have the society incorporated.

Section 49. Constitutions, Bylaws, Rules of Order, and Standing Rules

In preparing a constitution and bylaws, it's always a good idea to get copies of the ones used by similar organizations. The committee appointed to prepare the documents can then compare the copies and select the most appropriate one to use as a guide, amending each article of it (or each section or paragraph) just as the assembly will eventually amend the committee's report.

After the committee has amended the constitution it chose to use as a guide, it should adopt it as amended and go on to the bylaws, treating the bylaws the same way. After the committee is finished with both documents, someone should move to return to the assembly:

I move that the committee rise and that the [*committee*] chair [*or another member*] report the constitution and bylaws to the assembly.

If this motion passes, the documents are written out, and a brief report is made:

> **The committee, appointed to draft a constitution and bylaws, respectfully submits the following, with the recommendation that they be adopted as the constitution and bylaws of this society.**

The material offered may be signed by all of the committee members who agree with the reported version or just by the committee chair.

In the above example, it's assumed that both a constitution and bylaws are adopted. Some organizations, however, have only a constitution or only bylaws. When a group adopts both, the constitution will probably contain only the following:

- Name and purpose of the society

- Qualification of members

- Officers and their election and duties

- Meeting of the organization (but only including what is essential and leaving details for the bylaws)

- How to amend the constitution

These items can be arranged in five articles, with each article divided into various sections. Since a constitution has only fundamental information, an organization should make it very difficult to amend the constitution. Usually, a society requires previous notice of any proposed amendment and a two-thirds or three-fourths vote to adopt it (see Section 45); it's a good idea not to require a larger vote than two-thirds. When a group has frequent meetings, it shouldn't make an amendment except at a quarterly or annual meeting and then only after proposing it at the previous quarterly meeting.

The bylaws should contain all of the other rules of an organization that are too important to be changed without giving prior notice to all members about the proposed change, although the most important rules can be placed in the constitution rather than the bylaws. Or the bylaws might omit the rules about the conduct of business in a meeting and collect such rules in a separate document: the rules of order. In any case, every organization should have one rule in particular—either in its bylaws or in the rules of order:

> **The rules contained in [*name a selected book on parliamentary practice*] shall govern the society in all cases to which they are applicable and in which they are not inconsistent with the rules of order [*or bylaws*] of this society.**

Without a rule to that effect, someone could cause a lot of trouble in a meeting.

Standing rules are occasionally adopted by a society in addition to its constitution, bylaws, and rules of order. Such rules are permanent resolutions that are binding on the organization until rescinded or modified. Standing rules can be adopted by a majority vote at any meeting.

Once standing rules have been adopted, they can't be modified during the same session except by a motion to Reconsider (Sections 27, 60) them. But they can be suspended, modified, or rescinded by a majority vote at any future meeting. Standing rules, then, are rules that are adopted like ordinary resolutions with no need to give previous notice (required for bylaws) and so on. Members at any future session, therefore, may terminate them. No standing rule (or other resolution), though, can be adopted if it's in conflict with the constitution, bylaws, or rules of order.

The various types of rules are, unfortunately, mixed in some organizations, and that causes confusion. In other words, the standing rules really may be the bylaws if an organization doesn't allow them to be suspended or doesn't allow them to be amended without previous notice. This is a mistake. Standing rules should contain only those rules that are subject to the will of the majority at any meeting and those rules that it may want to change at any time (without having to give prior notice). Rules of order, on the other hand, should consist of only the rules pertaining to the orderly transaction of business at a meeting.

The rules of order, bylaws, and constitution should contain some provision for their own amendment, and the rules of order should also provide for their own suspension. The bylaws, too, might have a provision allowing for certain articles to be suspended (see Section 18).

Article X. Officers and Committees

Section 50. Chairman or President

The chair's duties include the following:

- To call the meeting to order at the appointed time

- To preside at all of the meetings

- To announce business before the assembly in its proper order

- To state and put to a vote all questions that are properly brought before the assembly.

- To preserve order and decorum

- To decide all Questions of Order (subject to an appeal)

If you're conducting the proceedings before a large assembly, when you put a question to a vote or speak in response to an appeal, you should stand; in all other cases you may remain seated. In meetings of boards, committees, and other small groups, though, the chair usually doesn't stand at all, and even members who are speaking keep their seats.

When you're conducting a meeting, you should observe these rules as well:

- Whenever a vote by the chair would affect the result or when the assembly is voting by ballot, the chair may vote also.

- When someone stands to speak and addresses you as chair (Mr. or Madam Chairman), respond by stating the person's name, if known, or by nodding to acknowledge the person.

- Don't interrupt a speaker as long as the person is in order but rather listen to the speech (which is addressed to the chair and not the assembly).

- Be careful not to appear to take sides while conducting a meeting, but you may call another member to take the chair while you address the assembly on some question.

- Don't leave the chair while speaking on a question or a matter of order.

People inexperienced in conducting a meeting should thoroughly study their organization's constitution, by-laws, and rules of order in advance and take copies along while occupying the chair. A presiding officer also needs to be able to answer members who ask what motion to make concerning some matter before the assembly (see Section 55). It's a good idea, therefore, to memorize the list of ordinary motions in their order of precedence and to become completely familiar with the table of rules (see list and table in the Quick-Reference Guide). The table can be scanned quickly during a meeting when you need to look up something you don't know offhand. In addition, while serving as chair, you need to know all of the business that normally comes before a meeting, and you must call for it in its regular order. Since it may be necessary to appoint new committees, you should also bring along a list of the members of all committees already existing.

Whenever someone makes a motion and it's seconded, you should immediately and distinctly state the question to the assembly:

The question is whether the chair should appoint a conference committee.

After a vote is taken, announce the result ("The ayes have it—the motion is carried") and state what question, if any, is pending at that time (see Section 54 for the proper form). But don't wait for routine motions to be seconded when you know that no one objects to them (see Section 65).

Sometimes a member unknowingly makes an improper motion. In that case, politely suggest the proper motion.

> *Example:* Suppose that someone moves to Lay [a question] on the Table (Section 19) until a certain time. Since that's an incorrect motion, ask the person if he or she means to Postpone [the question] to a Certain Time (Section 21). If the member says yes, announce that "the question is on postponement to [*time*]." On the other hand, if someone moves simply "to postpone the question" without stating a time, don't rule it out of order. But do ask the person if he or she wants to Postpone [the question] Indefinitely (Section 24), which would kill it, or to Lay [the question] on the Table, which means that it can be taken up at any other time. After the person tells you what he or she means, state the question that way.

> *Example:* Suppose that after a report has been presented and read, someone moves that "it be received." Ask if the person means to move "to adopt" or "to accept" it, since the report has already been received. (No vote is taken on *receiving* a report since that merely brings it before the assembly and allows it to be read—unless someone objects to receiving it; see Section 30.)

Although a committee chair usually has more to say than the other committee members, the chair of an ordinary deliberative assembly, especially a large one, has the least to say of all members concerning the merits of pending questions. But the chair of an assembly, nevertheless, controls the assembly in a fair and just manner. This means that as chair you would never interrupt members who are speaking simply because you know more about some matter than they do. Moreover, you would never let yourself get excited or respond unfairly to even the most troublesome member. Nor would you take advantage of someone's ignorance of parliamentary law even when you might temporarily accomplish something good by doing so.

As chair, you would need to know all about parliamentary procedure but shouldn't try to show off your knowledge. You should be careful not to be more technical or strict than is absolutely necessary for the good of the meeting. Above all, you should use your own best judgment in all situations. Perhaps an assembly would be hindered, not helped, by a strict enforcement of the rules. But in large assemblies in which there's a lot to do and always the potential for trouble, you would likely find that the safest course is to insist that the rules be strictly observed.

Section 51. The Clerk, Secretary, or Recording Secretary

The titles clerk, secretary, and recording secretary all refer to the same person. This individual keeps a record of the proceedings (minutes) at each meeting. How detailed the record must be depends on the type of meeting. In an occasional or mass meeting, for example, the record is usually very brief. But in any meeting the clerk should always record every resolution or motion that's adopted.

For a convention, it's often a good idea to keep a full record of the proceedings for publication. If the meeting lasts for several days it's best to appoint one or more assistant clerks to help. Deciding what to record can be a difficult task. Sometimes the main points of each speech should be written down. In other cases, it may be enough to write that a question was discussed by so and so in the affirmative and by so and so in the negative. Every adopted resolution, however, is recorded in full, for example:

> **the motion of Mr. Benson, it was resolved t . . .**

Sometimes the topics at a convention are assigned beforehand to certain speakers who make formal speeches during the convention. When a speaker finishes his or her subject, it's then open for discussion. People who want to discuss a subject will have some time limit, such as five minutes, to respond to the speaker's address. In such cases the minutes can be very brief—unless they're going to be published; then they'll have to include either the full addresses of the speakers or carefully prepared abstracts. Such detailed minutes would also have to show the drift of the members' responses to each subject.

In a permanent society, when the minutes aren't published, they consist of a record of what was done, not what was said. The recorded version is then kept in a minutes book. The secretary who keeps the minutes, regardless of detail, should never use them personally to make any criticism or even any favorable remarks about what was said or done in a meeting.

The minutes might be prepared in a form such as that shown here:

> *Example:* At a regular meeting of the XYZ Society, held in its hall, on Thursday evening, March 16, 19XX, with Ms. Addington presiding and Mr. Steinberg acting as secretary, the minutes of the previous meeting were read and approved. The Applications Committee reported the names of Jane Worley and Geoffrey Reynolds as applicants for membership. On the motion of Mr. Brighton, they were admitted as members. The Budget Com-

mittee reported through Ms. Purl two resolutions
that were thoroughly discussed, amended, and
adopted, as follows:

   RESOLVED, That . . .
   RESOLVED, That . . .

On the motion of Mrs. Harrison, the society adjourned.

                    Marilyn Foster, Secretary

When proceedings must be published, it's a good idea to
examine the published proceedings of other similar meetings and to try to conform to the established style or
custom, except when it's clearly improper to do so.

Put the constitution, bylaws, rules of order, and standing rules all in one book, leaving every other page blank.
Then whenever any article is amended, you can add the
amendment on the page opposite the original article.
Include on the page with the amendment a reference to
the date and page of the minutes in which the action of
the society pertaining to the amendment is recorded.

It's the secretary's job to keep all papers belonging to
the society that aren't specifically the responsibility of, or
assigned for safekeeping to, some other officer. Sometimes the secretary has financial duties, too (see Section
52).

Section 52. Treasurer

The treasurer's duties vary from one group to another.
Often the treasurer acts like a banker and merely holds
the funds the organization receives and pays bills on
order of the society signed by the secretary. The treasurer's annual report (always required) would then be merely
a statement of the amount on hand at the beginning of
the year, the amount received during the year (stating
the sources of the money), the total amount paid out by
order of the society, and the balance on hand. This

report next goes to the Auditing Committee, which consists of one or two persons. They examine the treasurer's books and vouchers and certify on the report that they have examined the accounts and vouchers and find them correct and that the balance on hand is so and so (stating the precise amount). When the Auditing Committee's report is accepted, it's the equivalent of a resolution by the society to the same effect—namely, that the treasurer's report is correct.

In the situation just described, the real financial statement would be made either by a board of trustees, the secretary, or some other officer, according to the requirements stated in the organization's constitution. The idea behind all of this is that any officer who receives money on behalf of an organization must account for it in a report, and the officer who's responsible for the disbursements must also report them to the organization. If the secretary is the one responsible for the expenses, which is the case in many societies, and the treasurer simply pays out on the secretary's order, the secretary should also be the one who makes a report of the expenses. This report should be prepared using appropriate expenses categories so that the society can easily see what things the various amounts of money were spent on.

The main purpose of a financial report, then, is to give members the information they want or are entitled to have. But all of the details, such as specific dates or separate checks written for the same purpose, would simply clutter a report and make it difficult to understand. The Auditing Committee, not all individual members of the society, is meant to examine such details.

Since an officer has to account for any money spent, it's important always to get a receipt for any payment. Keep such receipts in regular order, since they'll serve as the vouchers to be examined by the Auditing Committee. You can't be too careful where someone else's money is concerned. In fact, officers should *insist* on having their accounts audited every time they make a report so that any errors will be caught and quickly corrected. Once an organization accepts an Auditing Committee's statement that a financial report is correct, the officer who made the payments is relieved of responsibility for past accounting. In other words, if the payment vouchers were to get lost, it's not a problem in terms of past responsibility.

To decide what form of financial report to use for your organization, look at those prepared in similar societies. The example below can be varied to suit most cases.

Treasurer's Report

The undersigned, treasurer of XYZ Club, hereby submits the following annual report:

The balance on hand at the beginning of the year was ____ dollars and ____ cents. There was received from all sources during the year ____ dollars and ____ cents; during the same time the expenses amounted to ____ dollars and ____ cents, leaving a balance on hand of ____ dollars and ____ cents.

The attached statement of receipts and expenditures will show in detail the sources of receipts and the objects to which the expenditures were applied.

David Eggert
Treasurer, XYZ Club

You can make a Statement of Receipts and Expenditures simply by listing the receipts, followed by the expenses, and ending with the balance on hand. The Auditing Committee's certification about the correctness of the account should be written on the statement too, for example:

Dr.					Cr.
	The XYZ Club in acct., with David Eggert, Treas.				
19XX			19XX		
Dec. 31.	Rent room	$500.00	Jan. 1.	Bal. on hand from	
	Gas	80.00		last year's acct.	$ 21.13
	Stationery	26.50	Dec. 31.	Initiation fees	95.00
	Janitor	360.00		Members' dues	860.00
	Bal. on hand	24.63		Fines	15.00
		$991.13			$991.13

We do hereby certify that we have examined the accounts and vouchers of the treasurer and find them to be correct and that the balance in the account is twenty-four dollars and sixty-three cents ($24.63).

>FOR THE AUDITING COMMITTEE
>Jennifer Randall
>Lewis Samson

Section 53. Committees

Committees may not be needed in small assemblies, especially if they have little business to transact. But in large assemblies or meetings with a lot to do, committees are very important. When a committee is selected properly, its action will probably decide the action of the entire assembly.

A committee set up for action should be small and consist only of people who wholeheartedly support a proposed action. But a committee set up for deliberation or investigation should be large. It should represent all of the parties in an assembly so that its opinion will carry as much weight as possible. If some faction is left out or underrepresented, the committee won't be as useful. (See Section 46 on the appointment of a committee.)

The committee chair is the first person named to be on a committee. This person calls the committee together and presides at its meetings. Or a majority of the committee members may elect someone else to serve as chair, provided that the assembly hasn't already appointed the chair for them. If the committee chair is absent or simply fails or refuses to call a meeting, any other two members can call the members together for a meeting. Since the committee is a miniature assembly, it can act only when a quorum (see Section 43) is present.

When a paper is referred to a committee, the members must not write on it. Amendments by the committee

should be written on a separate sheet. If the paper originates in the committee, though, and doesn't come from
the assembly, all of the amendments by the committee
must be incorporated in the paper. Usually, when a
committee prepares the paper, someone from the committee drafts it in advance of the committee meeting.
The draft is then read paragraph by paragraph. After
each one, the committee chair asks:

> **Are there any amendments proposed to this
> paragraph?**

The committee doesn't vote to adopt each paragraph
as it comes up but rather waits until the whole paper has
been covered (paragraph by paragraph). Then the paper
as a whole is open to amendment generally, and at that
time the committee members can strike out any paragraph, insert new paragraphs, or even substitute an entirely new paper. As soon as the paper has been amended
to suit the committee, the members should adopt it as
their report and direct the committee chair, or some
other member, to report it to the assembly. The entire
paper should be written out, with the opening resembling
one of these examples:

> **The committee to which [*subject*] was referred
> submits the following report.**

> **Your committee appointed to [*object*] respect-
> fully reports as follows.**

The closing might begin:

> **This report is respectfully submitted.**

followed by the signatures of all committee members
who support the report or, perhaps, by only the signature
of the committee chair.

Sometimes the minority on a committee submits a
separate report. It might start by stating:

The undersigned, a minority of the committee appointed to [*object*], respectfully submits the following report.

The minority usually presents its report after the committee's report has been read. But the only way an assembly can act on a minority report is to move to substitute it for the report of the committee.

Once the committee's report has been read, the committee is automatically discharged without any need for a motion to that effect. However, the committee could be revived if someone would make a motion (and the assembly would adopt it) to refer the paper back to the same committee (to recommit).

Article XI. Introduction of Business

Section 54. How to Introduce Business

If you want to bring up some matter at a meeting, write it down (unless it's very simple) in the form of a motion, for example:

RESOLVED, That the thanks of this convention be expressed to the citizens of this community for their hearty welcome and generous hospitality.

At the proper moment—when no other business is before the assembly—stand up (in a large assembly) and address the chair by title (Mr. Chairman, Madam President, or the like). The chair should immediately recognize you, announcing your name (if known to the chair) or otherwise simply nodding to acknowledge you (it helps if members state their names right after addressing the chair). This means that you have the floor and can make your motion:

I move that we adopt the following resolution.

Or you might state that you want to "offer" the following resolution, read it, and then move that it be adopted. If the assembly is large, your name should be written on the resolution, especially if a lot of other business is being transacted at the meeting.

As soon as you've finished, hand your written resolution to the chair. Presumably, someone will second the motion (or the chair will ask if there's a second), and the chair will state the question:

It has been moved and seconded that the following resolution be adopted [*reads resolution*].

Or the chair could first read it and then state the question:

The question is on the adoption of the resolution just read.

That statement opens the resolution to discussion. Anyone who wants to speak, though, must first obtain the floor in the usual manner (address the chair and wait to be recognized).

But perhaps no one will rise or speak. At any rate, as soon as the chair thinks debate is closed, he or she asks:

Are you ready for the question [*or* "Is there any further discussion"; see Section 65]?

Again, if no one rises or speaks, the chair puts the question to a vote in a form similar to this:

The question is on the adoption of the resolution just read. Those in favor of its adoption say aye. [*Pause for yes vote*.] Those not in favor [*or* "those opposed"] say no.

After the no votes are in, the chair should announce the result, stating that the motion is carried or lost. If it carried, the chair might reply as in one of these examples:

The motion is carried—the resolution is adopted.

The ayes have it—the resolution is adopted.

A majority of the votes cast is enough to adopt any motion except those identified in Section 39. (For other forms of stating questions and putting questions to a vote, see Section 65; for other illustrations of the common practice in introducing business and in making various motions, see Sections 46–48.)

Article XII. Motions

Section 55. Motions Classified According to Their Object

Instead of adopting or rejecting a resolution immediately, the members might want to dispose of it in some other way. Certain motions can be used for this purpose while a resolution is being considered, and for the time being, those motions must be acted on first (if they qualify as taking precedence over the resolution; see list of precedence of motions in the Quick-Reference Guide). But no one may make any of these motions while someone else has the floor, except as shown in the table of rules (see Quick-Reference Guide).

Once a motion has been recognized by the chair as pending, it has to be disposed of by a vote, unless the mover withdraws it or unless the assembly adjourns while it's pending. It may be interrupted, however, by any motions that have precedence over it. But once those other motions are acted on, the members must resume consideration of the pending question (unless one of the other motions in effect settled the original matter under consideration). No new motion is necessary to bring the pending question back before the assembly. The members simply return to it as soon as the other motions are taken care of.

The following list shows most of the motions that can be made while another matter is pending. The motions are arranged here in eight categories according to the reason for wanting to make the motion.

Objective	*Motions to Accomplish Objective*
To modify or amend (see Section 56)	To Amend (Section 23) To Commit or Refer (Section 22)
To defer action (see Section 57)	To Postpone to a Certain Time (Section 21) To Lay on the Table (Section 19)
To suppress debate (see Section 58)	To call for the Previous Question (Section 20) To Limit Debate or Close Debate (Section 37)
To suppress the question (see Section 59)	To Object to Consideration of a Question (Section 15) To Postpone Indefinitely (Section 24) To Lay on the Table (Section 19)
To consider a question the second time (see Section 60)	To Reconsider (Section 27)
To apply orders and rules (see Section 61)	To call for Orders of the Day (Section 13) To make a Special Order (Section 13) To Suspend the Rules (Section 18) To raise Questions of Order (Sections 14, 61) To Appeal (Section 14)
To handle miscellaneous matters (see Section 62)	To request Reading of Papers (Section 16) To Withdraw a Motion (Section 17) To raise Questions of Privilege (Section 12)

To close a meeting   To Fix the Time to Which to
   (see Section 63)   Adjourn (Section 10)
                              To Adjourn (Section 11)

Section 56. To Modify or Amend

To amend. If you want to modify a question, the proper
motion would be to Amend (Section 23) by one of these
means:

- To add words

- To strike out words

- To strike out certain words and insert others

- To substitute a different motion on the same subject
  for the one currently before the assembly

- To divide the question into two or more questions to
  get a separate vote on some particular point(s)

Sometimes the opponents of a measure try to amend it
in such a way that the proponents will become divided
over it, thereby causing defeat of the measure.

When an amendment has been moved and seconded,
the chair should state the question distinctly so that the
members will know exactly what decision they have to
make. The chair, therefore, should first read the paragraphs being amended, next the words to be taken out (if
any), then the words to be inserted (if any), and, finally,
the paragraph as it will read if the proposed amendment
is adopted. As soon as the chair finishes reading, he or
she should state that the question is on the adoption of
the amendment and open the amendment to debate.
Comments at this point should be confined to the merits
of the amendment and shouldn't concern the main question unless it's necessary to discuss it to decide if the
amendment should be adopted.

The amendment itself can also be amended. But an
amendment of an amendment can't be amended further.

In other words, an amendment can itself be amended only once. None of the undebatable motions (see Section 35) can be amended except to Fix the Time to Which to Adjourn (Section 10), to Extend the Limits of Debate (Section 34), and to Close Debate or to Limit Debate (Section 37). The motion to Postpone Indefinitely (Section 24) also cannot be amended.

To Commit or Refer. Sometimes the original question is very complex, or perhaps it needs a more extensive amendment than the assembly can make. In such cases, someone should move to Commit or Refer (Section 22) it to a committee. You can make such a motion while an amendment is pending, and it opens up the whole merits of the question to debate. You also could amend such a motion by specifying the number of the committee, how the members will be appointed, when they'll report, or by giving any other instructions. (See Section 53 on committees and Section 46 on their appointment.)

Section 57. To Defer Action

To Postpone to a Certain Time. If you want to defer action on something until a particular time, the proper motion is to postpone it to that time. The motion to Postpone to a Certain Time (Section 21) allows only limited debate, and it has to be confined to the pros and cons of postponement to the specified time. You could amend this motion by changing the time; that amendment, though, would allow only the same limited debate. If you propose another time, it may not be beyond the *current* session (see Section 42); it may, however, be postponed to the *next* regular business session, at which time it will come up with the unfinished business and consequently take precedence over new business on that day (see Section 44). You can move for postponement to a certain time while another motion to Amend, to Commit, or to Postpone Indefinitely is pending.

To Lay on the Table. Instead of postponing a matter until a particular time, you might want to lay it aside temporarily while dealing with something else but still reserve the right to consider the matter at any time. In Congress the motion to Lay on the Table (Section 19) is commonly used to defeat a measure. A majority, however, may take it up again at any other time.

Some organizations won't allow a question to be taken up again except by a two-thirds vote to do so. Such a rule really deprives the group of the advantages of being able to lay something on the table. It wouldn't be safe to lay something aside temporarily because it might not be possible to get a two-thirds vote later to take it up again. A one-third minority, in fact, could easily dispose of a measure it didn't like by laying it on the table, knowing it would be unlikely that a two-thirds vote would be available later to call it back. In ordinary societies, a bare majority shouldn't have the power to adopt or reject something or to prevent others from considering it without debate. (See Section 35 on the principles involved in making questions undebatable.)

In any case, the way to put something aside temporarily is to move that the question be laid on the table. Since neither debate nor amendment is allowed on that motion, the chair would immediately put the question to a vote. If it passed, the matter would be set aside until the assembly voted to take it from the table. The motion to Take from the Table (Section 19) can't be amended, can't be debated, and doesn't have precedence over any other motions. Moreover, an affirmative vote on it can't be reconsidered. Sometimes this motion, too, is used to suppress a measure, as shown in Section 59.

Section 58. To Suppress Debate

Motions to suppress debate are strictly for closing or limiting debate. They may not be used by either friends or foes of a measure. Opponents of a measure could also close debate on it by suppressing the question itself (see Section 59).

Previous Question. If you want to force action on a debatable question, all you have to do is obtain the floor and call for the Previous Question (Section 20). After the call is seconded, the chair has to put the question to a vote right away because a call for the Previous Question can't be debated:

Shall the main question be now put?

After asking for yes and no votes, if this motion for the Previous Question passes by a two-thirds vote (see Section 39), all debate on the main question stops immediately, unless a committee member is in the midst of reporting the pending measure; anyone like that who has the floor is entitled to close the debate. In that case, as soon as debate stops, the chair "puts the question" to the assembly. If a motion to Commit (Section 22) is pending, the chair first puts that to a vote. If that motion carries, the subject goes to the committee; if it fails, the next vote is taken on any amendments and, finally, on the resolution as amended.

Suppose that the pending motion is one to Postpone Indefinitely (Section 24) or to Postpone to a Certain Time (Section 21) or to Reconsider (Section 27) or to Appeal (Section 14). Then the Previous Question is exhausted (no longer applies or has any effect) by a vote on a postponement, a reconsideration, or an appeal; that is, the Previous Questions, in that case, would no longer apply and, therefore, wouldn't cut off debate on any other motions that might be pending. Suppose, however, that the call for the Previous Question fails. If it does, the debate simply continues as though the motion for the Previous Question had never been made. You can also call for the Previous Question on an amendment. In that case, after the vote is taken on the amendment, the main question is once more open to debate. (Since the Previous Question is so generally misunderstood, reread Section 20 for further amplification.)

To Limit or Close Debate. Assume that you don't want to end debate completely. Then you wouldn't call for the Previous Question because that would stop everything and bring the matter to a vote. To simply limit debate (see Section 37), not kill it entirely, you could move to limit the time each person may speak or to limit the number of speeches on each side of an issue, pro and con. Or you could move to appoint a time when debate must close and the question has to be put to a vote. You also could move to limit debate on an amendment or on an amendment to an amendment. Afterwards, then, the main question would still be open to continuing debate and further amendment.

In ordinary organizations, where harmony is so important, a two-thirds vote should be required on any motion to cut off or limit debate. (The House requires only a majority vote to pass these motions. The Senate, on the other hand, doesn't even recognize motions to close or limit debate.)

Section 59. To Suppress the Question

Objection to the Consideration of a Question. Sometimes a resolution is introduced in an assembly that the members don't want to consider. Perhaps it's irrelevant to the objectives of the group or simply wouldn't be worth the time needed to deal with it. Whatever the reason, if you don't want to spend time on something, you should make a motion to the effect that you object to considering the question. An Objection to Consideration of a Question (Section 15) doesn't require a second, so the chair would immediately put the question to a vote:

Will the assembly consider this question?

After asking for yes and no votes, the chair would announce the result. If the members, by a two-thirds vote, decide they don't want to consider the question, it's dismissed right away and can't be introduced again during the current session. A key requirement in objecting to the consideration of a question, however, is that you do it when the question is first introduced, before it has been debated. You can make your motion even though someone else has the floor.

To Postpone Indefinitely. Once a question has been debated, there are two ways you can suppress it: defeat it with a no vote or move to Postpone [the matter] Indefinitely (Section 24). Both have the same effect. Even if the motion to Postpone Indefinitely should be lost, there's still a chance to defeat the resolution after an amendment has been voted on. Although you can't move to Postpone Indefinitely when another motion (other than the original or main question) is pending, you can do so after an amendment has been acted on and the main question, as amended, is before the assembly. The motion to Postpone Indefinitely opens the main question to debate just as if the main question itself were before the assembly. For that reason, though, you may need to call for the Previous Question (Section 20) to cut off debate and bring the matter to a vote.

To Lay on the Table. This motion is commonly used to suppress a question, but a two-thirds vote should be required to stop debate and suppress something (see Section 39). Suppose that there would be no chance of getting a majority vote during the rest of the current session to take up the question later. In that case, if you knew it wouldn't be taken up later in the session, a sure way of suppressing the question would be to get a motion passed to Lay on the Table (Section 19) that particular question. Since you can't debate a motion to Lay on the Table, the majority could immediately put the matter aside and be certain that it wouldn't be taken up again without majority consent.

Because of this motion's high rank (see precedence of motions list in the Quick-Reference Guide) and the fact that it can't be debated, it's commonly used to suppress a question. On the other hand, its effect is merely to put a matter aside until the assembly decides to consider it (see Section 57). It suppresses a question, therefore, only as long as a majority remains opposed to taking it up.

Section 60. To Consider a Question a Second Time

To Reconsider. There's only one way to consider a question a second time during the same session after it already has been adopted, rejected, or suppressed: You can move to Reconsider (Section 27) the vote on the question. However, to make the motion, you must have voted on the prevailing side (either for or against) when the question was first considered. Also, if the original vote isn't reconsidered on the day it was taken and no meeting is held the next day, it can't be reconsidered at the next meeting. (In Congress if "yeas and nays" [see Section 38] are not taken on a vote, anyone can move to Reconsider it. But yeas and nays are ordered on all important votes in Congress, something that isn't the case in ordinary societies.)

The motion to Reconsider a vote can be made and recorded in the minutes in the middle of debate even when someone has the floor (but it won't be acted on until later). The motion also can be made while another question is pending, although it can't be considered until there is no longer any other matter before the assembly. At that time, if the motion to Reconsider, which was made earlier, is called up, it takes precedence over every other motion except to Adjourn (Section 11) and to Fix the Time to Which to Adjourn (Section 10).

If you make a motion to Reconsider a vote on a debatable question, it will open to debate the entire merits of the original (debatable) question. But if the original question is undebatable, the reconsideration of the vote on it also will be undebatable. Whether or not a motion to Reconsider a vote on something opens the original subject to debate, therefore, depends on whether or not that original subject was debatable.

If a motion to Reconsider carries, the chair will state that the question is again on adopting the original question. This means that the original question is now treated as though no vote had ever been taken on it, and it, therefore, has to be voted on again before it can be disposed of.

Assume that you made a motion to Reconsider a vote on something and that your motion was therefore recorded in the minutes. But other business may have been before the assembly, so it couldn't be acted on immediately. Depending on the rules of your organization, you may not have to call it up that same day but may be able to wait for the next meeting *on a succeeding day*. This wouldn't be true, though, if your organization had no rule to allow this. If it didn't have such a rule and if your motion to Reconsider wasn't acted on before the close of the session when the original question was adopted, the motion would no longer have any effect.

Another possibility is that you decide not to call up the motion to Reconsider the same day as the original vote or even the next day—perhaps you have to leave and can't do so. If you don't do it on the succeeding day, anyone else may call it up that day. If there's no succeeding meeting (adjourned or regular) within a month, however, the effect of the motion to Reconsider will end with the adjournment of the meeting at which you made the motion. (This would be true of any other motion as well.)

The only way to consider a subject a second time, then, within the same session is to move to Reconsider the vote on the original question. This doesn't apply to a motion to Adjourn, but a motion to Adjourn can be renewed if business or debate has progressed; the vote can't be reconsidered, however. This rule doesn't prevent an assembly from renewing (see Section 26) any of the motions mentioned in Section 7 (subsidiary or secondary motions), if a question before the assembly has changed. In that case, although the motions may be basically the same ones, they are nevertheless technically different.

Example: To move to postpone a resolution is different from moving to postpone it after it has been amended, so the question now, being different as a result of the amendment, can be taken up again. A motion to Suspend the Rules (Section 18), though, can't be renewed at the same meeting, although it can be taken up again at an adjourned meeting. If a call for Orders of the Day (Section 13) is voted down, it can't be renewed while a question before the assembly is under consideration. (See Section 27 for many unusual aspects of this motion and Section 25 concerning the motion to Rescind.)

Section 61. Orders and Rules

Call for Orders of the Day. Sometimes an assembly decides that certain matters should be considered at a particular time. When that time comes, then, those questions are known as Orders of the Day (Section 13). If you were to call for the Orders of the Day, your motion would need no second, so the chair could immediately put the question to a vote:

Will the assembly proceed now to the Orders of the Day?

If the vote is yes, whatever subject is being considered must be put aside, and the questions that are supposed to be considered at that time are taken up in their assigned order. The chair, in fact, may not even wait for someone to make a motion but may simply announce the Orders of the Day without any vote, if no one objects. If someone makes a motion, though, and it fails, the motion can't be renewed until the subject presently being considered is first disposed of. (See Section 13 for a fuller explanation.)

Call for Special Orders. Sometimes a subject is so important that it's best to consider it at a special time even in preference to the Orders of the Day and any regularly established order of business. You could then move to make the subject a Special Order (Section 13) for that particular time. To be adopted, your motion would need a two-thirds vote because it's really a suspension of the rules. Such a motion would be in order, therefore, whenever a motion to Suspend the Rules would be in order.

If a subject is a Special Order for a particular day, on that day it supersedes all other business except for the reading of the minutes. A Special Order can be postponed, though, by a majority vote. If two Special Orders are made for the same day, the one made first takes precedence over the next one.

To Suspend the Rules. Every assembly that allows discussion needs rules to avoid a lot of wasted time and to help it accomplish its reason for being organized. Nevertheless, it's sometimes necessary to suspend the rules temporarily. To do this you can make a motion to Suspend the Rules (Section 18) that interfere with so and so. If your motion is carried by a two-thirds vote, you can then proceed with whatever you want to accomplish. But a vote isn't always necessary. By general consent (if no one objects), the rules can be ignored at any time without the formality of a motion and a two-thirds vote.

Questions of Order. The chair has to enforce the rules and preserve order. When you notice a breach of order, you can ask to have the rules enforced. First, address the chair:

Madam Chairman, I rise to a point of order.

The chair will then ask whoever is speaking to sit down and will listen to your comments. Having heard the point of order, the chair will make a decision and may let the person who was speaking continue—with a reminder to stop doing whatever was ruled to be out of order. But when a speaker has violated the rules of decorum, he or she may not continue if anyone objects without first getting the permission of the assembly through an affirmative vote. If someone is using improper language, you could also simply state:

I call the gentleman to order.

In that case, the chair, again, would decide if the language really is disorderly before letting the speaker continue.

To Appeal. Although the chair decides matters of order, interpretation of the rules, and priority of business, anyone can "appeal from the decision" of the chair. If you move to Appeal (Section 14) and your motion is seconded, the chair will first state again his or her decision and note the fact that it was "appealed from." Then the chair will state the resulting question:

Shall the decision of the chair stand as the judgment of the assembly [*or* "society, convention," *and so on*]?

Without leaving his or her seat, the chair can then give reasons for the decision and open the matter to debate (no one may speak more than once) unless it is undebatable, as in these cases:

- When it pertains to a violation of the rules of speaking, to some indecorum, or to the priority of business
- When the Previous Question (Section 20) was pending at the time the Question of Order was raised

After a vote is taken, the chair should state that the decision of the chair is sustained or reversed, as the case may be.

Section 62. Miscellaneous

Reading Papers and Withdrawal of a Motion. Suppose that you want to read a paper (see Section 16) or move to Withdraw a Motion (Section 17) that you made after it was stated by the chair. If anyone objects, it's necessary to make another motion requesting permission from the assembly to do so.

Question of Privilege. Assume that a disturbance occurs in a meeting or something else happens that affects the rights of the assembly or any of its members. You can then rise to a Question of Privilege (Section 12) and state the matter. After hearing your comments, the chair will decide whether it really is a matter of privilege. As usual, members can appeal the chair's decision.

If a question really is one of privilege, it supersedes, for the time being, the business before the assembly. There are several steps the assembly can take, however, to affect that status. You could make a motion to Postpone to a Certain Time (Section 21) the Question of Privilege. Or you could call for the Previous Question (Section 20), which would stop debate and bring the Question of Privilege to a vote. You could also make a motion to Lay [the Question of Privilege] on the Table (Section 19). Or you could move to Refer (Section 22) the Question of Privilege to a committee, which would examine it and report on it. In any case, as soon as the Question of Privilege is disposed of, the debate that was previously in progress resumes.

Section 63. To Close a Meeting

To Fix the Time to Which to Adjourn. When you want to have an adjourned meeting of an assembly, make a motion before it closes:

> That when this assembly adjourns, it adjourns to meet at ___ time.

You can amend such a motion by changing the time. But if you make the motion when another question is before the assembly, neither the motion to Adjourn nor the amendment can be debated. On the other hand, if you make the motion when nothing else is before the assembly, it stands the same as any other main question and thus can be debated. You could make a motion to Fix the Time to Which to Adjourn (Section 10) even while the assembly is voting on a motion simply to Adjourn (Section 11). But you could not make that motion when someone else had the floor.

To Adjourn. An assembly might be kept in session an unreasonably long time if an organization didn't have a rule to limit the time each person could have the floor. (Ten minutes are allowed by Robert's rules of order.) When you want to end a meeting, then, you either have to wait for someone speaking to yield the floor or have to wait until the person's time is up. As soon as the floor is available, you should move to Adjourn (Section 11). After there's a second, the chair will immediately put the question to a vote, since no amendment or debate is allowed. If the vote is affirmative, the chair will state:

The motion is carried; this assembly stands adjourned.

If no other meeting is forthcoming, the chair should state:

The motion is carried; this assembly stands adjourned without day [*sine die*].

If earlier it was decided that the assembly would adjourn to meet at a particular time, the chair would state:

The motion is carried; this assembly stands adjourned until [*time*].

Suppose that you want to qualify a motion to Adjourn by stating a time (to adjourn to tomorrow evening). In that case, you must wait if another question is before the assembly since that motion stating the time, like any other main motion, can be amended and debated. (See Section 11 for the effect of an adjournment on unfinished business.)

Article XIII. Miscellaneous

Section 64. Debate

In debate you always direct your remarks to the chair, stick to the question before the assembly, and avoid any focus on personalities or comments about someone else's motives. Permanent assemblies usually adopt rules limiting the number of times any person can speak on the same question and how long the speech may be. (The House allows one speech of one hour per member. The Senate allows two speeches of any length per person.) If there weren't some time limits in debate, a person could defeat a measure by prolonging his or her speech and by refusing to yield the floor (except for a motion to Adjourn).

In ordinary assemblies, each member should be allowed two speeches (except on an Appeal [Section 14]). Robert's rules also limit the time to ten minutes per speech. A member may speak more often or longer if the assembly gives him or her permission by a two-thirds vote. The motion requesting such permission can't be debated.

Suppose that an assembly wants even more freedom in debate. It could then consider a question informally or form a committee of the whole (see Sections 32 and 33). Or an assembly might want greater limits. In that case, debate could be restricted more or even stopped completely by a two-thirds vote (see Section 58).

Section 65. Form of Stating and Putting Questions

When a motion is made and seconded, assuming the motion is in order, the chair will state the question to the assembly. A second to a motion is required when it's necessary to ensure that a person introducing something isn't the only one in favor of it. In other cases such as routine matters or questions that clearly are supported by many, a second is usually not needed, and the chair just assumes that the motion is "seconded."

In routine work, the chair often puts the question to a vote without even waiting for a motion. Few people like to make such formal motions, and a lot of time would be wasted waiting for them. But the chair can do this only if no one objects. A presiding officer also can save time by not taking a vote on a routine question. The chair, therefore, might announce that if there's no objection, so and so will be considered the action of the assembly. After a treasurer's report, for instance, the chair might state:

> **If there's no objection, the report will be referred to an auditing committee consisting of Ms. Webster and Mr. Lopez. [*Pause to see if anyone objects*.] It is so referred.**

These motions do not have to be seconded:

- Call for Orders of the Day (Section 13)
- Questions of Order (Section 14)
- Objection to Consideration of a Question (Section 15)

A common form of stating a question is this:

> **It has been moved and seconded that [*motion*].**

Another common form is as follows:

The question is on [*subject of motions*].

With resolutions, one might state (after they were read):

The question is on the adoption of the resolutions just read.

Sometimes, to be very clear, the chair should not merely repeat the motion but should also state that the question is on its adoption. With an Appeal, the chair would first state the chair's decision (and, if appropriate, the reasons for it) and state that the decision has been appealed from and then state the question:

The question is, shall the decision of the chair stand as the judgment of the assembly?

In putting the question to a vote, the chair would state the question and add:

Those in favor of sustaining the decision of the chair say aye. [*Pause for vote.*] Those opposed say no.

If the ayes have it, the chair should announce the result in one of these forms:

The ayes have it, and the decision of the chair stands as the judgment of the assembly.

The decision of the chair is sustained.

In stating the question on an amendment, the chair should read:

- The passage to be amended
- The words to be struck out, if any
- The words to be inserted, if any
- The whole passage as it will stand if the amendment is adopted

After that, the chair would state the question, for example:

> **The question is, shall the word *censure* be inserted in the resolution in place of the word *thanks*?**

As soon as a vote is taken, the chair should immediately state the question (if any) that is again before the assembly. In other words, if the assembly has just voted on an amendment, the chair would announce the result and then state:

> **The question is again on the resolution [*or* "on the resolution as amended"].**

If an amendment is reconsidered, the chair should announce the result of the vote and state the question before the assembly in a form such as this:

> **The motion is carried—the vote on the amendment is reconsidered. The question is again on the adoption of the amendment. [*See Section 31 about acting on committee reports and on papers with several paragraphs.*]**

After stating the question on a motion that can be amended or debated, the chair should pause to see if anyone immediately rises or speaks and, if not, ask:

> **Are you ready for the question?**

The form in some societies:

> **Are there any remarks [*or* "further remarks"]?**

When the chair believes the debate is closed, he or she would again ask:

> **Are you ready for the question?**

If no one rises or speaks this time, the chair will state the question once more and immediately put it to a vote. One of the most common forms of putting a question to a vote (after it has been stated again) is this:

> **Those in favor of the motion say aye [*or* "hold up their right hands"]. [*Pause for vote.*] Those opposed say no [*or, again,* "hold up their right hands"].**

See Sections 38, 46–48, and 54 for examples of various ways to state questions and put them to a vote. See the Quick-Reference Guide for unusual forms.

Part III. Miscellaneous

Article XIV. Legal Rights
Section 66. Right of Deliberative Assemblies to Punish Members

A deliberative assembly has an inherent right to make and enforce its own laws and punish offenders. The most extreme penalty it may impose, however, is expelling a member from its own body. If the assembly is a permanent society, it may (for its own protection) give public notice that the offender is no longer a member of its organization.

But a society may not go beyond what's necessary for self-protection. It may not, for example, publish the charges against an expelled member. In one such case, an officer of a society published—on order of the society—a statement of the serious charges of which a member had been found guilty. The expelled member then brought a libel suit against the officer and recovered damages after the court had ruled that the society erred and that it didn't matter whether the charges were true.

Section 67. Right of an Assembly to Eject Someone from a Meeting

A deliberative assembly has the right to decide who may be present during a session. When an assembly decides by rule or vote that someone may not remain in the room, the chair has to enforce that rule or order, using whatever force is needed to remove the person.

When someone must be taken out of a meeting, the chair can direct other members to remove the person without calling the police. The members doing this, however, should be careful not to use harsher treatment than is necessary. The courts have held previously that anyone who is unnecessarily harsh is liable to prosecution the same as any member of the police force would be under the same circumstances. Nevertheless, however badly a person may be abused by another member while being removed from a room, neither the chair nor the society itself will be liable for damages. They merely ordered the removal, which does not exceed their legal rights.

Section 68. Rights of Ecclesiastical Tribunals

Many deliberative assemblies are ecclesiastical bodies, and it's important to know to what extent civil courts will respect their decisions. One interesting case went to the U.S. Supreme Court.

Example: A church became divided, and each party claimed to be the church; each one, therefore, also claimed to be entitled to the church property. The case first went to the civil courts and, finally, on appeal, to the Supreme Court. The Court held it under advisement for a year before reversing the decision of the state court. That decision was based on the fact that the state court ruling conflicted with a decision of the highest ecclesiastical court that had acted on the case.

In its decision, the Supreme Court laid down this broad principle: When a local church is only part of a large and more general organization or denomination, the court will accept as final the decision of the highest ecclesiastical tribunal to which the case had been carried within that general church organization. It won't inquire into the justice or injustice of its decree in regard to the parties before it. The officers, ministers, members, or church body that are recognized by the highest judiciary of the denomination will also be recognized by the court. When the church body expels or cuts off any members, therefore, the court also will hold that they're no longer members of that church.

Section 69. Trial of Members of Societies

Since a deliberative assembly has the right to expel someone, it also has to have the right to investigate the character of its members. It can require that any member must testify in a case or, upon refusal to do so, may be expelled.

Charges against a member's character are usually referred to a committee of investigation or discipline or to some standing committee. The committee then has to report its findings to the organization. Some societies have standing committees formed to report any disciplinary cases that arise.

In matters of discipline, a committee's report to the society doesn't have to go into detail but should give recommendations for action that the society should take. It usually would close with resolutions covering the case, so there shouldn't be any need for someone else to offer additional resolutions. When the recommendation is expulsion, the ordinary resolutions are as follows:

- To fix the Time to Which to Adjourn (Section 10)

- To instruct the clerk to cite the member to appear before the society at the adjourned meeting, where the member will show cause why he or she should not be expelled in view of the charges

• To list the charges against the member

After charges have been brought against a member and an assembly has ordered that the person be cited to appear for "trial," the member is theoretically "under arrest." He or she is deprived of all rights of membership until the case is resolved. Without a member's consent, though, the individual shouldn't be tried at the same meeting at which the charges were preferred unless the charges relate to something done specifically at that meeting.

It's the clerk's duty to send the accused person a written notice to appear before the society at the appointed time. At the same time the clerk should give the accused individual a copy of the charges. If the accused person doesn't obey the summons, the society usually considers that act cause enough for summary expulsion.

The trial takes place at the appointed meeting. Often the only evidence required is the committee report. The committee chair or someone else from the committee then reads the report and offers any additional evidence that the committee wants to introduce. After that, the accused person should be allowed to give an explanation and introduce witnesses. Each party should be allowed to cross-examine the other's witnesses and introduce rebutting testimony. As soon as all evidence is in, the accused should leave the room, and the society should consider the question. Finally, the society should vote on the question of expulsion or any other proposed punishment. No one should be expelled, however, by less than a two-thirds vote, with a quorum voting. (The U.S. Constitution [Article 1, Section 5] provides that each house of Congress may, "with the concurrence of two-thirds, expel a member.")

There's a vast distinction between the evidence needed to convict someone in a civil court and that required to convict an accused person in an ordinary society or an ecclesiastical body. A notorious pickpocket, for instance, couldn't even be arrested let alone convicted in a civil court simply because he or she was known as a pickpocket. But that would be enough "evidence" for an ordinary society to convict and expel someone. Moral belief in the truth of some charges against a member is all that an ecclesiastical or other deliberative body needs to find the person guilty of the charges.

If a trial is likely to be long and troublesome or very delicate, the accused person is often cited to appear before a committee instead of the society itself. The committee would then report the results of its trial of the case. This would include resolutions covering the punishment it recommends that the society adopt. After the committee report has been read to the society, the accused person should be allowed to make a statement, and the committee should be allowed to reply. When that's over, the accused individual leaves the room, and the society acts on the committee's resolutions. Committee members would vote on the case the same as the other members.

An accused person might ask to be represented by counsel at the trial. If so, a society would usually allow this, although the counsel would have to be a member of the society in good standing. But if the counsel is guilty of improper conduct during the trial, the society could refuse to hear any more and could also punish that person.

Section 70. Call of the House

A call of the house is an order that compels absent members to attend a meeting. But it's a process that's allowed only in assemblies that have a rule providing this power. (A call doesn't apply in voluntary societies.) Usually, when no quorum is present, a small number (one-fifth of the members-elect in Congress) can order a call of the house.

In the early history of Congress a call of the house required a day's notice. In the English Parliament it's customary to order a call for a certain future date, usually not over ten days later, although it has been as long as six weeks later. The object is to give notice so that all members may be present on that day when important business is scheduled to come up. In Congress a call nowadays is used only when no quorum is present. As soon as a quorum appears, further proceedings in the call (see the explanation in Section 70 under "*Proceedings in a Call of the House*") are usually dispensed with, and this is in order at any stage of the proceedings. In some legislative bodies, though, proceedings in the call can't be ignored unless a majority of the members-elect vote to do so. In Congress it's customary after the call to pay the fees that were assessed for being absent.

To prevent an assembly from using a call improperly, it's a good idea to provide that when the call is made, the members can't adjourn or dispense with further proceedings in the call until a quorum is obtained. A rule such as that in the following example would work in city councils and similar bodies that have the power to enforce attendance:

Example: When no quorum is present, members may order a call of the house and compel the attendance of absent members. After the call is ordered, a motion to adjourn or dispense with further proceedings in the call cannot be entertained until a quorum is present or until the sergeant-at-arms reports that in his or her opinion no quorum can be obtained that day.

If a quorum isn't present, a call of the house takes precedence over everything, even the reading of the minutes, except for the motion to Adjourn (Section 11). To take effect, a call requires an affirmative vote for it by the number specified in the organization's rule (one-fifth, for example). If the rule allows for a motion making a call while a quorum is present (for the purpose of getting a larger attendance), the call should rank with Questions of Privilege (see Section 12) and require a majority vote to be adopted. If a call is rejected, it shouldn't be made again while a quorum is present at that meeting (see Section 42).

After a call is ordered and until further proceedings in the call are dispensed with, no motion is in order except one to Adjourn or another motion relating to the call. A recess, then, couldn't be taken by unanimous consent. An adjournment ends all proceedings in the call, although before the adjournment, if a quorum is present, the assembly can order arrested members to make their excuses at an adjourned meeting.

Proceedings in a Call of the House. When the call is ordered, the clerk calls the roll alphabetically and notes which members are absent. The clerk then calls the names of just the absentees, at which time explanations of absence can be requested. (Congress usually excuses members who have "paired off," which refers to two members on opposite sides of a pending question who have both agreed to stay away. But the absence of both members must not affect the result, which would rarely happen in municipal bodies.)

After the roll call and the excuses, the doors are locked, and no one may leave. An order similar to the following is adopted:

That the sergeant-at-arms take into custody and bring to the bar of the House such of its members as are absent without leave of the House.

A warrant is signed by the presiding officer and attested by the clerk with a list of absentees attached. This is given to the sergeant-at-arms, who immediately "arrests" the absent members.

According to House Rule 22: "It shall be the duty of the Sergeant-at-Arms to attend the House during its sittings; to aid in the enforcement of orders, under the direction of the Speaker; to execute the commands of the House from time to time; together with all such process, issued by authority thereof, as shall be directed to him by the Speaker." The words *sergeant-at-arms* can be replaced in the order by *chief of police* or whatever officer is designated to serve the process.

The sergeant-at-arms then appears with various members under arrest, goes to the chair's desk (after being announced by the doorkeeper in large bodies), followed by the arrested members, and returns to his or her post. The chair "arraigns" each member separately and asks what excuse each has for being absent from the assembly without leave. Each member gives an excuse, and someone moves that the person be released from custody and allowed to take a seat either without paying a fee or after paying the required fine. But until a member has paid any fees assessed for the absence, he or she can't vote or be recognized by the chair for any purpose.

Quick-Reference Guide
to Motions

A LARGE PART of meeting conduct concerns *motions*—statements that participants make to introduce business or to propose something requiring a decision, or vote. *Webster's Ninth New Collegiate Dictionary* describes a motion as "a proposal for acting," especially "a formal proposal made in a deliberative assembly." For a decision to be reached, then, someone has to "make a motion" proposing it. Since this activity is predominant in most meetings, the 1893 *Robert's Rules of Order* appropriately provided a quick-reference table of rules about motions, similar to the one given here. According to General Robert, this table capsules data that will enable you "to decide some two hundred questions of parliamentary law without turning a page." The rules table provides the following information:

- An index to the various sections in the book that discuss each motion in detail (refer to the section numbers along the left column of the table where the motions are listed alphabetically)

- A classification of the various motions according to whether they (1) are debatable, (2) open main questions to debate, (3) cannot be amended, (4) cannot be reconsidered, (5) require a two-thirds vote, (6) do not need to be seconded, (7) are in order when another person has the floor (refer to the asterisks [*] in the seven columns of the table to see which rules, if any, apply to each motion)

- A determination of the motions to which the above seven categories apply *in part* (refer to the notes to the table and the corresponding note numbers in each of the seven columns)

Two additional lists follow this table:

1. Precedence of Motions (which ones are more important) and whether they can be amended or debated and what vote they require (such as a two-thirds vote to pass)

2. Forms of Putting Certain Questions (the correct formal wording to use to state a motion and ask for a vote on it)

How to Use the Table during a Meeting

When you're in the middle of a meeting, you don't have time to start reading a book of rules or to page through such a book to hunt for various sections. The following tables and lists are meant to provide fast answers. For example, assume that you're conducting a meeting and someone makes a motion while another motion is pending. Glance at the Precedence of Motions list to see if the second motion is in order (a lower-rank motion, for example, can't supersede one of a higher order). Then look for the motion in the left column of the Rules about Motions table. Check the adjacent seven columns in the table for asterisks and footnote numbers. If there are no asterisks in the columns, you know that:

- The motion is debatable.
- The debate must be strictly confined to the motion.
- The motion can be amended.
- The motion can be reconsidered.
- The motion must have a majority vote to be adopted.

- The motion must be seconded.

- The motion is not in order when another person has the floor.

An asterisk in one of the columns, however, means that the motion is an exception to the general rule. A note number in the column refers to one of the notes to the table that explains to what extent it is an exception.

> *Example:* Imagine that you're conducting a meeting and that an amendment of a resolution is before the assembly and someone makes a motion ("moves") to Refer it to a committee ("to Commit"). First check the Precedence of Motions list, where you will find that "to Commit" is in order—it stands above "to Amend." Next, check the table of rules, where you will discover that the motion differs from an ordinary resolution because it "opens to debate the main question" (the original resolution). If someone then moves to "Postpone [the question] Indefinitely," you should rule it out of order according to the Precedence of Motions list (it's of *lower* rank than "to Commit"). On the other hand, if someone moves "to Lay [the question] on the Table," you would find that it takes precedence over "to Commit" and is in order (it's of *higher* rank). The table of rules would then immediately clarify the seven pertinent points (or rules) for you. (To learn more about how to find such information in the table, refer to the Explanation at the top of the table.)

By checking the lists and the table (including notes and the introductory Explanation) you can quickly decide how to handle motions as they're made in a meeting. Eventually, if you conduct very many formal meetings, you'll no doubt want to memorize the rules about the most common motions. But for the others, a quick-

Rules about Motions

Notes

1. Every motion in this column has the effect of suspending some rule or established right of deliberative assemblies (see Section 39) and, therefore, requires a two-thirds vote, unless a special rule to the contrary is adopted.

2. Undebatable if made when another question is before the assembly.

3. An amendment may be made either (a) by adding or (b) by striking out words or paragraphs or (c) by striking out certain words and inserting others or (d) by substituting a different motion on the same subject or (e) by dividing the question into two or more questions as specified by the mover so as to get a separate vote on any particular point(s).

4. An appeal is undebatable only when relating to indecorum (see Section 36) or to transgressions of the rules of speaking (see Sections 34, 36, 64) or to the priority of business or when made while the Previous Question is pend-

Explanation: The left column of the table lists the various motions alphabetically and gives the number of the accompanying section in the text discussing the motions. The seven column headings are the main rules that apply to motions. An asterisk [*] in one of the seven columns means that the rule described in the column head applies to the adjacent motion in the left column. A note number means that the rule only partially applies, and the extent to which it applies is described in the note itself. For example, "Lay on the Table" is a motion discussed in Section 19 of the text. Asterisks in two columns show that it's undebatable and can't be amended. Note 5 indicates that an affirmative vote on this motion can't be reconsidered. The other four columns are blank, meaning that the motion does *not* "open the main question to debate," does *not* "require a two-thirds vote," *does* "need to be seconded," and is *not* "in order when another member has the floor."

Section	Motion	In order when another member has the floor (§2)	Does not require to be seconded (§3)	Requires a two-thirds vote (§39). See n.1.	Cannot be reconsidered (§27)	Cannot be amended (§23)	Opens main question to debate (§35)	Undebatable (§35)
11	Adjourn				*	*		*
10	Adjourn, Fix the Time to Which to							2
23	Amend (n. 3)							
23	Amend an Amendment					*		
45	Amend the Rules			*				
14	Appeal, relating to indecorum etc. (n.4)	*				*		*
14	Appeal, all other cases	*						
14	Call to Order	*	*			*		*

	Motion							
37	Close Debate, motion to						*	
22	Commit or Refer						*	
34	Extend the Limits of Debate, motion to							*
10	Fix the Time to Which to Adjourn	2						
36	Leave to Continue Speaking after Indecorum					*	*	
19	Lay on the Table					*	*	
37	Limit Debate, motion to				5	*	*	
15	Objection to Consideration of a Question (n.6)					*	*	*
13	Orders of the Day, motion for the					*	*	
21	Postpone to a Certain Time	7						
24	Postpone Indefinitely						*	
20	Previous Question (n.8)			*			*	
44	Priority of Business, questions relating to			*			*	
12	Privilege, Questions of							*
16	Reading Papers			*		*		
27	Reconsider a Debatable Question	9		*		*		
27	Reconsider an Undebatable Question	9		*	*			
22	Refer (same as Commit)							
25	Rescind							
11	Rise (in Committee: Adjourn)				*		*	
13	Special Order, to make a							*
23	Substitute (same as Amend)					*	*	
18	Suspend the Rules					*	*	
19	Take from the Table					*	5	
44	Take up a Question Out of Its Proper Order					*	*	
17	Withdrawal of a Motion			*			*	

ing. When an Appeal is debatable, only one speech from each member is permitted. On a tie vote the decision of the chair is sustained.

5. An affirmative vote on this motion can't be reconsidered.

6. The objection can be made only when the question is first introduced, before debate.

7. Allows but limited debate upon the propriety of the postponement.

8. The Previous Question, if adopted, cuts off debate and brings the assembly to a vote on the pending question only, except where the pending motion is an amendment or a motion to Commit, when it also applies to the question to be amended or committed.

9. Can be moved and entered on the record when another person has the floor but can't interrupt business then before the assembly; must be made on the day or the day after the original vote was taken and by one who voted with the prevailing side.

reference table is indispensable. However, don't rely on the table alone. Before you conduct a formal meeting, *read the text of this book* describing the rules of order and the organization and conduct of business. Those text sections will help you to become familiar with terminology such as "lay the question on the table," to learn what the duties of the various officers and committees are, and to become adept at managing debates and other meeting activities.

Precedence of Motions

The following list shows the rank of ordinary motions. Any motion (except to Amend) can be made while another *lower*-rank motion is pending. But no motion can supersede another motion of *higher* rank. The motion calling for the Previous Question requires a two-thirds vote; all others need only a majority.

Motions	Can Be Amended	Cannot Be Amended
Undebatable Motions		
To Fix the Time to Which to Adjourn	X	
To Adjourn (*when unqualified*)		X
For the Orders of the Day		X
To Lay on the Table		X
The Previous Question (*requires two-thirds vote*)		X
Debatable Motions		
To Postpone to a Certain Time	X	
To Commit or Refer	X	
To Amend	X	
To Postpone Indefinitely		X

The motion to Reconsider can be made when any other question is before the assembly. But it can't be acted on until the other question is disposed of (see note

9 to table) when, if it's called up, it takes precedence over all other motions (except to Adjourn and to Fix the Time to Which to Adjourn). Questions that are incidental to those before the assembly take precedence over them and must be acted on first.

Forms of Putting Certain Questions

"Putting a question" is parliamentary terminology for placing a motion before an assembly for a vote. Various sections in the text describe common formal and informal forms for stating a question and putting it to a vote, and the following are examples of unusual forms:

- To demand the Previous Question is to move that debate cease and the assembly vote on the pending question(s). The formal wording by the chair is: "Shall the main question be now put?" or "Shall debate be now closed and a vote taken on the pending question [*or* 'resolution' *or* 'amendment']?" See Section 20.

- To Appeal from the decision of the chair is to object to a decision. The chair would reply: "Shall the decision of the chair stand as the judgment of the assembly [*or* 'society, convention, board,' *and so forth*]?" See Section 14.

- To call for the Orders of the Day is to ask to have the assembly conform to its designated order of business. If the chair fails to announce business in the proper order and orders are called for, the chair may ask: "Will the assembly now proceed to the orders of the day?" See Section 13.

- When a question is introduced and someone voices an Objection to Consideration of the Question, the chair asks: "Will the assembly consider it?" or "Shall the question be considered [*or* 'discussed']?" See Section 15.

- Voting may be by ballot, show of hands, roll call, general consent, or voice. If the vote is ordered to be taken by "yeas and nays" (by voice; see Section 38), the chair may state: "Those who are in favor of adopting these resolutions will, when their names are called, answer yes [*or* 'aye']. Those opposed will answer no." (See Section 38.)

27 million Americans can't read a bedtime story to a child.

It's because 27 million adults in this country simply can't read.

Functional illiteracy has reached one out of five Americans. It robs them of even the simplest of human pleasures, like reading a fairy tale to a child.

You can change all this by joining the fight against illiteracy.

Call the Coalition for Literacy at toll-free **1-800-228-8813** and volunteer.

Volunteer Against Illiteracy. The only degree you need is a degree of caring.